Sus
GH(
&
LEGENDS

Tony Wales

COUNTRYSIDE BOOKS
NEWBURY, BERKSHIRE

First Published 1992

COUNTRYSIDE BOOKS
3 Catherine Road
Newbury, Berkshire

ISBN 1 85306 209 X

Cover Design by Mon Mohan
Produced through MRM Associates Ltd., Reading
Typeset by Paragon Typesetters, Deeside, Clwyd
Printed by J W Arrowsmith Ltd., Bristol

Introduction

BEFORE the advent of modern mass-produced entertainment, story-tellers were highly valued members of the rural community. Their stories ranged from tales of recent times, perhaps featuring characters well known to the audience, to old favourites as ancient as time, which could be repeated again and again without complaint. These were the stories which today we call legends – hallowed and refined by time, often with a supernatural element, and with vague (sometimes very vague) connections with real events. But it must be conceded that most legends had at least some factual basis, even if of a very insubstantial nature.

The folk memory can be long and tenacious, and it is not unreasonable to suppose that the stories of dragons and strange beasts began as accounts of the prehistoric creatures that once roamed the heavily wooded Sussex weald. Equally, tales of fairies can be equated with memories of a race of shy, little folk who, like the monsters, have completely disappeared. The Devil, as taught by the early Christian church, was a real personage, waiting to pounce upon the souls of the unsuspecting and simple Sussex folk; so it is not surprising that he features in many of our tales and legends, although he is usually denied his conventional name.

The smuggling era in the South East undoubtedly gave a great impetus to the spread of folk stories featuring some sort of supernatural element; the object being to discourage inquisitiveness after nightfall.

Although many of our best legends now remain only as memories of the past, surprisingly others refuse to die and still persist in the popular imagination, in spite of competition from all the trappings of 20th century materialism.

In this collection I have tried to bring to life some of the best Sussex legends, including many little known ones. But I should emphasise that this is only a sampling and should in no way be considered comprehensive; in fact some of the best known tales have been purposefully omitted this time.

There are ghosts a-plenty, as these feature in so many traditional, and indeed modern, folk tales. The Sussex countryman's obsession with the supernatural appears to be as strong today as in the past. There are also the things of which legends are made – smugglers, hermits, eccentrics and even a rhyme and song or two.

I hope readers who enjoy this sort of patchwork of Sussex folklore will forgive me if a favourite legend, or village, is not represented. By all means write and tell me if so, and who knows, perhaps next time . . .

Tony Wales
July 1992

ADVERSANE

FAIRS are often featured in Sussex tales and legends. Although but a village, little Adversane had an important fair each year on September 12th, with as well as the usual side-shows and cheap-jack's stalls, many horses, cows and pigs offered for sale.

Mr E Carley, son of Gaius Carley, the famous Sussex blacksmith, recalled the fairs as very large with at least two roundabouts, and with a pig being roasted on a spit as the centre of attraction. There were lots of horses involved in transporting the larger pieces of fair equipment, so blacksmiths like his father had plenty of work. The fair often ended in fights, with Police Sergeant Trott having to be fetched from Horsham to sort things out.

One year a local shepherd beat the professional boxer in the popular fight booth, and when the proprietor refused to pay up, a second fight ensued. Again the local man triumphed, and went home with his money. A party of gypsies were said to have laid in wait for him, taking his prize money and killing him at the same time. Presumably these were not the fair people, who would not have been gypsies, but a separate gang who had watched the proceedings and decided to turn it to their advantage.

The tree under which he was murdered became known as The Shepherd's Oak, and so a local legend was born, as it soon became known as a very haunted spot. Eventually the tree was struck by lightning, and so the story came to an end.

Another murder victim was believed to haunt a spot on the lane between Adversane and Broadford Bridge. The ghost was of a sailor who had been drinking away some of his pay at the Blacksmith's Arms. He bragged loudly about how much money he was carrying, and this was his undoing, as the murderers waylaid him, taking his life for the sake of the cash.

ALDRINGTON

NOW part of Hove, the village of Aldrington once had an anchorite – a holy hermit who dwelt in a cell adjoining the old church of St Leonard. Most anchorites were men or women who, forsaking the pleasures of the world, resolved to spend their lives in solitude and prayer. This was no easy decision, as permission had to be obtained from the bishop, and the hermit was then ceremoniously incarcerated in what was almost a living tomb. In the case of Aldrington, the bishop's permission was probably even more difficult to secure, as the person concerned was the parish priest, the Rev William Bolle, who was appointed rector some time before 1397. We will never know what events led him to make the decision to resign his living and become an anchorite. But resign he did, taking his vows of seclusion in Chichester Cathedral in 1403. His cell was said to be 24 ft wide and 29 ft long, close to the lady chapel of the church, to which he had access. Perhaps because of his previous connection with the church, the normal rules were relaxed somewhat, as he apparently said mass in the church at certain times. Of course like all anchorites, he was dependent upon the local population for food and alms, but who was able to provide this is not clear, as it must have been a rather lonely place. He lived until at least 1415, as in this year Bishop Rede left him a bequest in his will. Later he apparently moved to a cell close to the cathedral church at Chichester, where there must have been many more pilgrims to contribute to his wellbeing.

By the 16th century it was said that the church at Aldrington was so neglected that it had no door, and the rector removed the font to his own house to prevent it being stolen. By the following century there were only eight or nine parishioners, and the church bell was reputedly 'stolen' by the village of Henfield. In 1831 there were only two parishioners, the toll-gate keeper and his wife. The man afterwards lost his wife, and also one of his legs, so strictly speaking the population was then only three-quarters.

ALFRISTON

LIKE many other Sussex churches, Alfriston church has a legend attached to it involving the Devil (or some other evil force). The original foundations of the church were laid in a field called Savyne Croft on the north side of the village. Each night invisible hands hurled the building blocks over the houses and into the Tye, a piece of common ground. Eventually the builders gave in (they nearly always did!) and the church was built there in the form of a cross, following the advice of a local wise man. This was suggested by the position of four oxen who were lying asleep on the spot.

The lovely church has been given the title of 'the Cathedral of the South Downs'. It has another interesting item of traditional lore attached to it, as it was here that the old custom of making virgin's garlands for the funerals of unmarried young women (and sometimes even young men) was carried out, probably the last place in Sussex where this was done, as the tradition does not appear to be known at any other place in the county.

Alfriston has a well known ghost story, concerning the heir to the Chowne Estate, who was out for an evening stroll with his dog, when he was ambushed by a gang of rogues who attacked him with clubs, the intention being to rob him. They went too far, and he was killed, the dog suffering the same fate when it tried to protect its master. The ghosts of young Chowne and his dog were said to appear every seven years. In the 19th century White-Way Road was being widened, and the navvies cutting away the hillside found the skeleton of a young man, presumed to be the murdered heir. The skeleton was given decent burial, and the ghost ceased to appear.

In his book *Our Sussex Parish,* Thomas Geering gives part of a song about the White-Way ghost. This is an unusual example of a local supernatural legend being commemorated in song:

When evening closes in with shadows grey,
And the ghostly vapours overhang White-Way,
And the crescent moon hangs gloomy in the west,
'Tis then the spirit of young Chowne can't rest,
But walks abroad with melancholy stride,
Adown the path that skirts the chalk-hill-side.

ANGMERING

THIS is a story about a curse, but unlike most stories of this sort, this one has a happy ending. It concerns the manor of West Angmering, which had a curse placed upon it by French nuns. The manor had been owned by the Abbey of Fecamp, but was seized by Edward IV. The belief was that no male heir would be born in the manor until it was returned to its rightful owners, the French. In the 18th century it was acquired by a Scot whose wife gave him 14 children; presumably some of these were males, so the curse did not seem to be working very well by that time. The nicest part of the story is that after the First World War, the owners bequeathed it to the daughters of Marshall Foch, so the house was finally returned to French ownership.

ARLINGTON

THE original bells of the church of St Pancras, Arlington, are said to lie at the deepest part of the river, known as Bell Hole. The missing bells can only be retrieved by six pairs of flawless white oxen, and although several attempts have been made, all have been unsuccessful. In every case, right at the last minute one of the oxen was found to have a small amount of black on his hide.

One of many Sussex bell legends, and as we shall see in other entries in this book, it has a very familiar theme (similar legends crop up in other counties). Often these legends have a witch or wise man involved in the attempt to retrieve the bells, but as far as Arlington is concerned, no such character appears in the tale.

ARUNDEL

ARUNDEL must surely be one of the most romantic and legendary towns in Sussex. The very sight on the skyline of castle, church and cathedral is sufficient to stir any imagination into thoughts of heroic deeds and supernatural beings. Arundel's most famous legends centre around its own particular giant – Sir Bevis, born of the great Sir Guy of Southampton and a Scottish Princess.

So great was Bevis in stature that he was easily able to wade across the Solent from the Isle of Wight, just for mere enjoyment. One day be spied the castle, and going to the earl he offered to be his warden in return for an ox, a Southdown sheep, two barrels of ale and as much bread and mustard as he liked, as his weekly rations.

His horse was of course just as mighty as he himself, and his staff was considered worthy of exhibition in Bosham church, although in more recent times it seems to have disappeared. On his 100th birthday, he decided he had lived long enough, and calling for his squire, he requested that his great sword, known as Morglay or Mongley, should be brought to him. This he flung with a mighty heave, decreeing that where it fell would be the place of his burial. It fell at Pugh Dean in Arundel Park, and buried itself in the grass by a mound, which is now pointed out as Bevis's Grave. Other reasons why we should not doubt his existence, are provided by Bevis's

Tower, which is part of the castle, and his great sword which may still be seen. There is also Bevis's Thumb – a long barrow above the Mardens, close to the Hampshire border.

Those born in Arundel have the right to call themselves 'Mullets'. The word actually refers to a type of fish, long regarded as a delicacy, which could be caught in the river Arun at Arundel. It is one of the traditional 'seven good things of Sussex'. A rhyme which evidently originated in neighbouring Offham runs thus:

Arundel mullet – stinking fish,
Eat it off a dirty dish.

The reply from the Arundel side was equally rude:

Offham Dingers, churchbell ringers,
Only taters for your Sunday dinners.

As might be expected in such a place, Arundel has many ghosts. Several have been seen in the parish church of St Nicholas. A figure of a nun, dressed in a grey habit, was seen twice in the 1940s by the town crier, who went to the church to wind the clock regularly in the evenings. The girl was seated in a chair, and after a few minutes she just vanished, chair and all. Nine months later he saw exactly the same figure. This was on the stairway landing of the bell tower. Behind the landing was a heavy oak door, leading on to a small timber platform, which may have been used as a lookout point during the Civil War. The doorway was afterwards blocked up, and the ghost then ceased to make an appearance. It has been conjectured that a young nun from the nearby convent might have fallen or jumped from the platform.

Another church ghost has been seen only on a photo, taken around the same period by an amateur photographer, who had no idea that he was capturing anything unusual on his film. The picture, which has been reproduced several times, shows the shadowy outline of what appears to be a priest wearing a chasuble, in front of the altar.

Yet a third ghost was seen by a church worker, and

could even be the aforementioned nun noted by the town crier, but in a different place. This was also a woman in grey, in a position of prayer in a pew in the adjoining Fitzalan chapel (separated from the parish church by a glass screen). The man called his wife, and she saw it also, until it gradually dissolved as they watched.

It must go without saying that the castle also has its ghostly visitors. A young girl has been seen near one of the towers, from which legend says she flung herself after an unfortunate love affair.

'The Blue Man' appears only in the castle library, bending over a book as if reading it. He is dressed in the clothes of the time of Charles II.

In the kitchens, the pots and pans are known to rattle at night, as if someone is hard at work. Occasionally the thunder of artillery from the siege of 1643 can be heard within the castle.

Not surprisingly, the family have a death token in the form of a strange white bird, which is said to flutter at the windows when a member is about to die. It should be stated that many old and historic families have a similar belief.

ASHINGTON

THE French have a legend which tells of animals of a dazzling whiteness which appear only at night, and vanish as soon as anyone attempts to touch them. Mrs Charlotte Latham writing in 1868 gives an account of a supernatural happening which reminded her very much of the French 'fetiches'. A blacksmith's wife at Ashington was found one morning very much disturbed in mind, and when questioned she said that she was sure of bad news before the day ended, because the previous night when waiting for her husband to return late from Horsham, she saw something rather like a duck, but a great deal whiter, in fact whiter than any snow. She cried out at it, and the thing went off faster than she had ever seen anything run before. When it was suggested to her that it could have been a cat with the moonlight shining on it, she denied the possibility, saying that such white things were sent as warnings, and that she would hear of a death before night. Whether she did receive such grisly news is unfortunately not related.

BALCOMBE

FOR an unexplained reason, Balcombe village traditionally carried on a feud with Cuckfield. When the people of Balcombe wanted their church spire to rival the much grander one at Cuckfield, they are supposed to have planted manure around the base to make it grow.

One of many similar rhymes in Sussex, tells the tale in this way:

Balcombe folk, what silly people,
Built their church without a steeple.

Could it have been Cuckfield folk who first chanted this rhyme?

A well known Balcombe ghost story from Victorian times concerns a local curate and his lady friend who, when out walking across the fields, saw a man's body hanging from a tree at the end of a cart rope. They went to tell the local policeman, but when they returned the man had vanished. Talking about their experience they found that there was a local legend telling of how a poor man had hanged himself at that spot, and his ghost had continued to make an appearance every now and then. At least six other people claimed to have seen the apparition. Another twist sometimes added is that the tree was subsequently struck by lightning, but when the suicide was 're-enacted', the tree appeared whole and entire.

Leslie Fairweather in his book on Balcombe, published in 1981, tells another, less well known, Balcombe ghost story.

The main character is a soldier on sentry duty at the important Balcombe rail tunnel during the Second World War. After a number of bombs had fallen nearby, he took refuge inside the tunnel. To his surprise three men approached him, and he challenged them. Getting no response, he tried again, and then they became faint, finally vanishing completely.

Recounting his story later, he was told that during the First World War, three soldiers had been killed by a train just inside the entrance of the tunnel, in fact right at the spot where he had been standing.

BARLAVINGTON

THIS tiny village, near Petworth, once had an infamous witch known as 'Old Sue Redding'. She was dreaded, feared and in a sense respected by all the poorer folk, and even many of the better educated. Witches are not usually connected with smugglers, but Sue Redding was reputed to keep up a chain of communications from her cottage with smugglers on the south coast. Dread of her evil powers kept folk away from her dwelling at night, but there were plenty of rumours concerning what went on there, between her and the smugglers.

She was known as a fearless horsewoman, riding always without saddle or bridle. Farmers were expected to allow her the use of their horses whenever it pleased her, and most did so out of fear. Their carters would tell them that if they did not allow their horses to be borrowed by Sue, then they would be found to be 'hag-rid' by the morning. When she was allowed the use of a certain horse, it was said to be refreshed, rather than tired afterwards.

One particular farmer stood out against her, and dared to deny her requests. One night when out in a fearful storm, he saw a hare sitting at the crossroads, looking completely serene and composed in spite of the weather (witches are always mixed up with hares). His mare would not go forward, and suddenly he found himself unhorsed, never recovering completely from the fall. Needless to say, he never jeered at Old Sue Redding again.

BEXHILL

A SUSSEX magazine carried an account in 1939, of the experience of a man who slept in a small room on the top floor of a Bexhill house in the summer of 1930. He awoke early one morning to behold a phantom, less than 2 ft away from the bed. It was of a big and powerful man dressed from head to foot in dazzling gold and silver chain armour. His eyes were covered by a visor, his nose was long and large, and he had large white teeth. He appeared to be smiling.

On his neck he wore an enormous chain of a very elaborate design, and hanging from it was a large black cross with a big agate in the centre. After a very few minutes, the phantom disappeared.

The narrator had been unable to find any story or explanation to account for the ghost.

BOGNOR REGIS

ALTHOUGH Brighton was particularly renowned for its bathing attendants, Bognor had a beach celebrity also, although a little later on. This was Mary Wheatland, affectionately known as 'Our Mary'. Born in 1835, she began her career at 14 hiring out costumes, giving swimming lessons and looking after the cumbersome bathing machines which were at that time a very necessary part of the process of swimming in the sea. Many stories and legends grew up around her, as she was undoubtedly a great character. She always dressed in a long serge dress, disapproving of more skimpy bathing wear, although this never seemed to cause her any problems. She would often dive off the end of Bognor Pier, or even stand on her head in the water waving her buttoned-up boots in the air. She retired at 71, with the proud claim that no bather had ever drowned on her part of the beach.

BRAMBER

ALTHOUGH only a part of the castle remains, it has kept its ghosts. The most dramatic is the sight of four young children holding out their hands for food. They are said to be the children of the De Braose family, captured by King John and held as hostages, in a feud which was carried on to the bitter end. The children were incarcerated and starved to death, and in Victorian times villagers claimed to have seen them, particularly at Christmas time. When anyone summoned up the courage to speak to them, they disappeared.

Two other castle ghosts are Maud of Ditchling and her lover William de Lindfield. When Maud's husband, Lord Hubert de Hurst, found them embracing in the garden, he was so enraged that he had the young William locked in a dungeon in the castle, keeping his guilty wife in suspense as to the whereabouts of her lover. Giving William just enough food and drink to keep him alive, he built up a wall day by day, until he finally entombed the unfortunate man, leaving him to starve to death in darkness. Just before he died, Maud was allowed by her husband to hear William's moans, but her entreaties that he should be freed were in vain. She died of a broken heart soon afterwards, and legend has it that the cruel Lord Hubert also died at the same time, a raving lunatic at the last. Many years after, a skeleton was discovered, crouching in a corner, head upon hands, elbows upon knees.

Yet another castle ghost is of a white horse which gallops round the dried-up moat on moonlit nights.

BREDE

A VERY unpleasant legend tells of Old Oxenbridge, also known as 'The Ogre of Brede'. Old Oxenbridge had an appetite for the flesh of children; in fact he liked one every night for his supper. After enduring his wicked ways for long enough, the children of Sussex met together and decided on a plan. They contrived to dope him with strong drink, and having rendered him senseless, they proceeded to saw him in half with a wooden saw – the children of West Sussex on one side and those of East Sussex on the other. All this took place in Stubb's Lane, between Brede Place and the church, at a spot since known as Groaning Bridge. This is said to be haunted by a ghost of the giant in the form of a sawn tree trunk.

There is some doubt as to which member of the Oxenbridge family the legend is about, although Sir Goddard Oxenbridge, who lived in the 16th century, is generally regarded as the one. However, this seems most unfair, as history records that he was actually a good and generous man and a devout Christian, who now lies in effigy in Brede church. The statue is quite small, whilst the legendary ogre is reputed to be of great size. But it has been pointed out that the size of the statue does not really mean anything, as statues were often made to a much smaller scale than the person represented. In fact Edmund Austen in his book *Brede, The Story of a Sussex Parish* (1946) tells how an old inhabitant remembered some excavations being made in the Oxenbridge chancel which revealed a skull of abnormal size.

Smugglers used the story of the ghost to scare villagers away from their unlawful activities, so this does cast considerable doubt on the origin of the ghost story. Mothers of naughty children were said to use the image of the ogre to frighten them into better behaviour.

To add further weight to the story of the Brede giant, Brede Place has the alternative name of The Giant's House. There were several other ghost stories connected with the house, including one of a priest who once used the chapel. But the smugglers may have had something to do with these also.

BRIGHTLING

SPIRITS were abroad in the mid 17th century in Brightling (accounts vary as to the exact date). A local man and his wife were much troubled by dust and dirt being thrown over them, even when in bed. Their house was set alight, and after several such attempts, the whole place was burnt down. They were then forced to move to another house, but similar disturbances continued, and then this house was also destroyed by fire. None of their neighbours were at all anxious to offer them accommodation, so they were forced to take refuge in a hut. However, dishes, knives and brickbats continued to fly about their heads.

Finally the man confessed to having been a thief, and to make matters worse some of his thieving had been carried out on Sundays. He then named the articles which he admitted he had stolen.

The confession seems to have had little effect, and the disturbances went on. Mr Bennet, minister of Brightling church, endeavoured to exorcise the spirits with prayers, but still to no avail. Neighbouring ministers then joined with him, and proclaimed a Fast Day, on which sermons were preached in all the churches in the area. Attendances were reported to be very great, and the congregations 'diligently attentive'.

The sequel to this affair was that a servant girl eventually confessed that she had been in conversation with an old woman, suspected of being a local witch, in which she had been told that many calamities would befall her master and mistress – but if she spoke of this, the Devil would tear her to pieces.

Most of the above has the appearance of a typical example of poltergeist activity, and we even have the young servant girl at the end of the tale, who could have been the focus for such activity. We are told that after her confession, the disturbances ceased.

BRIGHTON

THERE were a great many Brighton ghosts, but the one with the most unusual name was undoubtedly 'Olde Strike-a-Light'. His haunt was The Rising Sun inn close to the beach. It is not known when this inn was established, but it was evidently one of the earliest inns opened in the town. The original name was The Naked Boy, and on the sign over the front door was a picture of a naked child, with a roll of cloth under his left arm and a pair of shears in his right hand. Beneath the figure was the wording:

So fickle is our English nation,
I would be clothed if I knew the fashion.

Around 1755/60 the host, Mr Thomas, altered the sign to the more conventional Rising Sun.

Because it was so close to the beach, the inn would have afforded a very convenient place for smugglers to deposit their goods, and for this reason it has been suggested that 'Olde Strike-a-Light' may well have been invented, as were many other similar legends, to prevent prying eyes from seeing what they were not supposed to see.

However we will not spoil a good ghost story, but with the author of *A Peep into the Past* in 1892, look into the cellars of the old inn, which as he pointed out may indeed have convinced many of the supernatural horrors said to be connected with them. On the east side of the main cellar, a ponderous door opened into the wine cellar, about six ft in length and three or four ft wide. As could be seen by the dim light, there was fungi growing plentifully from its blackened roof. But beyond this cellar was another recess, to which the light failed to penetrate. It was of much smaller proportions (about three ft by two ft), which intensified all the gloom and repulsiveness of the preceding cellar. Here there was a mass of fungi growing in huge pendants of nearly a foot in length, covered in filth and festooned by spider's webs. The floor consisted of just one huge stone slab, from whence tradition said a large amount of money was dug, and whence 'Olde Strike-a-Light' would emerge wearing miller's garb. Later it was said that a number of human bones had been recovered from this spot, together with a sword, the point of which could never be cleaned because of the blood on it when it was buried.

The best known legend about 'Olde Strike-a-Light' concerns the Jervoise family of Brighton. Swan Jervoise was returning by boat one night, when he was amazed to see tremendously bright lights streaming from every window of The Rising Sun. He beached his boat and went ashore, knocking and bawling at the door of the inn. Unable to rouse the landlord, he was about to break open the door, when the lights again burst from the windows, each time accompanied by the sound of flint being struck by steel. The next moment the door opened and he was confronted by a figure seven ft high, wrapped in a black cloak and with a high conical white hat. Poor Swan Jervoise was transfixed with terror, and all he could do was shriek. The landlord heard his cries and came down with a torch, and seeing nothing amiss, comforted him as best he could. Left alone for a few moments, Jervoise began to recover from his fright, and was then plunged into greater terror as the tall ghostly figure made a reappearance, and pointed to the hearth. This was more than he could take, and he swooned senseless to the ground. The next day he repeated the tale to Father Anselm of St Bartholomew, and then, tragically, expired. The hearth was subsequently examined, and a vast treasure was discovered. After that time the inn was no longer troubled by the spirit of 'Olde Strike-a-Light'.

This well-constructed story was not agreed upon by all the locals. Many other details were forthcoming, such as the fact that the ghost's dress was not black but white, and that when he appeared he would seat himself astride a barrel in the cellar, clinking money in a pewter dish. One thing they all seemed to agree over was that he liked to strike lights with flint and steel, the flashes of which could often be seen far out to sea. There was also the question of who benefited from the treasure, the general opinion being that it was the couple Shaky and Nanny Bradford who had taken over the house from Mr and Mrs Thomas, before the appearance of the ghost. The fact that they were able to retire comfortably-off was considered good evidence that they had found 'the crock of gold'.

Other classic Brighton ghosts included the 'Wick Woman' who haunted the gap which formerly ran down to the beach from Lansdowne Place, and who plagued the boys who were on their way to bathe. There was also 'Betsy Bedlam' who, when Regency Square was known as Belle Vue Fields (with a capstan in its centre), was the terror of the children of this area.

Then we must not forget 'The White Hawk Lady' of Race Hill, who was supposed to have been the ghost of Editha Elmore, daughter of a rich squire of Woodingdean. She met a violent death on the Downs, and has haunted the spot ever since. In 1884 it was reported that she had been joined by a male companion, and that when they were watched, they would slowly fade away.

In St Nicholas' old parish churchyard, on certain nights a ghostly white horse gallops around the church, the site of which in pre-christian times was reputed to have been crowned by a circle of great stones. This could have been a pagan place of worship, and certainly several large stones have been found in the locality. The Brighton folklorist Miss L N Candlin conjectured that the white horse was a pre-christian sacrificial animal.

Early in this century many tales were told about the white horse, including that it had acquired a ghostly rider, and that its bones had been found when the first electric light cables were being put in. White horses were supposed to bring good luck to Sussex folk. A Sussex rhyme went:

White horse, white horse,
bring me some luck.
Spit three times,
and that's enough.

But you had to take care not to look back at it once it had passed you, or that would change the luck to misfortune.

Lillian Candlin of Brighton told of an old lady named Brown who used to stand opposite the old Chain Pier, holding a basket full of lucky necklaces made of small holed stones, which she gathered from the beach in the winter, cleaning and polishing them, and threading them on ribbons to be taken home by holidaymakers as souvenirs. They were of course taking home a very ancient form of good luck charm. Victorian children chanted:

Lucky stone, lucky stone,
Bring me some luck.
Today or tomorrow,
By twelve o'clock.

Holed stones were often hung up by the side of a cottage door for luck, and were also used by white witches as a charm against ague. Even today, visitors on Brighton beach are sometimes delighted to find a holed stone, looking upon it as a sign of luck.

In the late 19th century there still existed in Brighton an old custom carried out by the fishermen, who were always great custodians of old beliefs and observances. This was known as bending-in, and consisted of a meal of bread and cheese, or bread and treacle given by the fishermen before commencing mackerel fishing, to any children who were on the beach. Amusement in the form of Punch and Judy was also sometimes provided, and the children then wished the fishermen good luck as they commenced their labours. When casting the nets, the Brighton fishermen stood with their hats off, and said the following prayer:

There they goes, then; God Almighty,
Send us a blessing, it is to be hoped.

As each barrel (120 nets) was cast overboard, they said:

Watch barrel, watch. Mackerel for to catch.
White may they be, like a blossom on a tree.
God send thousands, one, two and three,
Some by their heads, some by their tails,
God send thousands, and never fails.

When the last was overboard, the master said 'Seas all'. If he had said 'Last Net', he would not have anticipated seeing his nets again.

As the vicar of Brighton was entitled to a share in the

profits of the fishing boats, one can understand how a blessing was once bestowed upon the fishermen before they commenced work. It has, with considerable logic, been surmised that 'bending in' is a corruption of 'Benediction', which in pre-reformation days would have been provided by the priest for the fishermen of his congregation, probably giving them communion - thus creating the tradition which now exists as a meal of bread and cheese.

No collection of Brighton tales and legends would be complete without something on Henry Cope, Brighton's famous 'Green Man'. His antics in the early 19th century even found him a place in the newspapers of the day. For instance on October 6th 1806, the *Lewes and Brighthelmston Journal* reported 'The Green Man continues daily to amuse Steine promenaders with his eccentricities'.

A typical account of him tells us that he dressed in green pantaloons, green waistcoat, green frock, green cravat, and his countenance, although powdered, was no doubt also green from the reflection of his clothes. He ate nothing but green fruit and vegetables, his rooms were painted green, with a green sofa, green chairs, green table, green bed, and green curtains. His gig, his portmanteau, his gloves and of course his whip were all green. A green silk handkerchief, and a large watch fastened with green seals, completed his outfit. It was generally agreed that he came of a good family, and that he always behaved like a gentleman. A contemporary poet described him thus:

A spruce little man, in a doublet of green,
Perambulates daily the streets of the Steine,
Green stripes is his waistcoat, his small clothes are green,
And oft round his neck a green kerchief is seen.

Green watchstring, green seals, and for certain
I've heard,
(Although they're powdered) green whiskers, and Eke,
a green beard.
Green garters, green hose, and deny it who can,
The brains too are green, of the little green man.

As the poet implied, he was odd to the point of insanity, as was proved by a subsequent jump from the top of the cliff opposite South Parade, to the beach 20 ft below. The story goes that when he was carried back to his apartments, his intellect was so impaired, that he had to be forcibly restrained from further foolhardy acts. This is the last we hear of the strange Mr Cope, so it must be assumed that he ended his tragic life in some kind of institution.

One other of Brighton's famous characters, whose life was one long legend, was Phoebe Hessel, who kept a stall near the Steine for several years, selling apples, bull's eyes and gingerbread. She was a recognised celebrity in her black poke bonnet and black cloth coat over a white apron, and a pair of men's boots. At the celebrations to mark the fall of Napoleon in 1814, Phoebe as Brighton's oldest inhabitant, then aged 101, sat beside the vicar of Brighton. She was also at the coronation celebrations of George IV, by this time 107 and blind. She died in 1821, having seen almost the whole of the 18th century, and part of the 19th.

But all that was only the epilogue to what had been a most remarkable life. The story is told briefly on her gravestone in the churchyard of St Nicholas:

> 'In memory of Phoebe Hessel who was born in Stepney in the year 1713. She served for many years as a private soldier in the 5th Regiment of foot in many parts of Europe and in the year 1745 fought under the command of the Duke of Cumberland at the Battle of Fontenoy, where she received a bayonet wound in her arm. Her long life commenced in the time of Queen Anne. Extended to the reign of George IV by whose munificence she received comfort and support in her later years. She died in Brighton where she had long resided. December 12th 1821. Aged 108 years.'

The story of a woman fighting under the guise of a male soldier has long been a favourite with story tellers and ballad singers. One can just imagine how Phoebe's story as recounted by herself, must have earned her much fame and even a deal of financial support in her old age; in fact George IV when Prince Regent, who knew how to be generous, allowed her a pension of £18 a year, and called her 'a jolly old fellow'. However it has to be stated that grave doubts have been cast on her story, and it does seem possible that as she grew older so her exploits were embellished with additional details – and after all who was left to contradict her.

In the 18th century sea bathing was enjoying an enthusiastic bout of popularity, and the Brighton fishing families were only too ready to supplement their normal incomes by providing attendants and instructors for those who were less used to the water. The male attendants were called 'bathers' and the women 'dippers' (possibly from the term used for attendants at mineral-water spas).

Several of these were great characters and gathered around themselves many legendary tales, some of which may have been true, and some perhaps not. The most famous of the women 'dippers' was Martha Gunn, who flourished in her chosen profession for nearly 50 years. Born in 1727, her early years are unrecorded, but from the middle of the century she made a name for herself as one of the most sought after ladies in Brighton.

With all his faults, the Prince Regent had the gift of mingling easily with all classes, and Martha, although only 'the queen of the dippers' was reputedly a great favourite of his. She is said to have had many friends among the servants in the royal kitchen, and was not above pocketing a few perks on her regular visits. One day the Prince was visiting 'below stairs' and noted with amusement Martha secreting a pack of butter within her spacious gown. Engaging her in conversation, he gradually edged her nearer and nearer to the cooking stove. The heat quickly melted the butter, resulting in the embarrassed lady standing in a pool of yellow fat. This was just the sort of slightly crude joke that 'Prinny' thoroughly appreciated.

In her day Martha was considered very much a local celebrity, and she even sat for a portrait with the equally famous 'Green Man'. She died in 1815, and around 40 of her friends are said to have taken part in the funeral procession, which was attended by many of the townsfolk.

A contemporary rhyme said it all:

There's plenty of dippers and jokers,
And salt water ripe for your fun,
The King of 'em all is Old Smoaker,
The Queen of 'em all Old Martha Gunn.

As this rhyme implies, Martha's opposite number was Smoaker Miles, the 'bather' who looked after the men. Like her, he was a local celebrity, and was credited with being able to swim 'like a mackerel'. Smoaker had a particular reputation as a strong minded man who would brook no nonsense from anyone, be they prince or pauper. In spite of, or perhaps because of this, he was said to be a great favourite of the Prince Regent, who delighted in rough hewn characters. Once, when the sea was more boisterous than usual, the Prince declared his intention of bathing as usual. 'No, no, Mr Prince. It is too dangerous' said Smoaker. 'But I will' said the Prince, making for the bathing machines. 'Come, come. This won't do' was the reply. 'I'll be damned if you shall bathe. What do you think your father would say to me if you were drowned . . .' The Prince laughed, and wisely heeded his advice.

On another occasion when the Prince ventured further into the waves than Smoaker felt was prudent, he seized the royal ear, and pulled him unwillingly to the shore. When his royal charge remonstrated, he is supposed to have replied with an oath or two, and the remark 'I arn't agoen to let the King hang me for letten' the Prince of Wales drown hisself'.

The affection was evidently not one-sided, as Smoaker actually walked all the way from Brighton to London during winter to visit the Prince Regent at Carlton House where he was well received. When too old to carry on his work as a 'bather' he was given a pension by the Prince. He died aged 74 in 1794, universally liked and respected for his blunt sincerity.

BROADWATER

AT Broadwater, once a separate entity but now virtually part of Worthing, there was an old oak known as 'The Midsummer Tree'. On Midsummer's Eve six skeletons were said to rise up from its roots and dance around the tree until daybreak.

Mrs Charlotte Latham, writing in 1868 about lingering West Sussex superstitions, mentioned one young man who had been detained at Findon on business very late, and forgetting it was Midsummer's Eve, had been frightened out of his very senses by seeing the skeletons capering. Several other people confirmed his story.

BULVERHYTHE

BULVERHYTHE, now part of outer Hastings, has one of the many Sussex bell legends. As at Bosham, the bells are said to be beneath the sea, and ring out mysteriously without human aid. But the bells are only heard when the weather is very bad, and local fishermen connect this with hearing the sea making a raking noise on the beach, which is always considered a sign of even more bad weather to come.

BURWASH

IN 1633 Thomas Nevitt, who was described as a citizen and draper of London, left to the parish in memory of his wife Obedience, gifts to the poor, and fees to the parson for preaching sermons. Obedience was the daughter of Robert Cruttenden of Burwash and her husband thought so well of her that he not only left money in her memory, but also had a tablet erected in Burwash church and a monument in London.

In 1633 the fund for the parson's sermons amounted to £2 10s charged on lands in Romney Marsh. Later the parson's fees were given to the poor, and in 1857 amounted to £3 6s 1d. In 1987 it was converted from perpetual payments into annual payments of £290 for twelve years, and is divided between St Bartholomew's, and St Philip's, Burwash Weald.

Much fascinating country lore relating to Burwash and other places in Sussex may be found in a gem of a book *Sussex Folk and Sussex Ways* written by the Rev John Coker Egerton, who was rector of Burwash in the late 19th century.

BURY

BURY once had a witch, who the villagers declared could turn herself into a white hare, and who communed with the Devil. This was probably the same woman who Mrs Latham in her *Some West Sussex Superstitions Lingering In 1868* tells about. Young girls would consult the witch to find out if their future husbands would be short or tall, poor or rich, or dark or fair. Some would walk a long distance in order to talk to the witch.

Bury folk were probably no more superstitious than most village dwellers in past centuries, but by 1948 some of the younger ones were becoming more blasé about such things. Lilian Brown in her book *All about Bury* tells of a local boy who was walking to Amberley station to meet his grandmother who was returning late from Littlehampton. He said he must go to the station as his grandmother would not walk past Bury Combe alone at night, because of the ghost. The supposed haunting of the Combe was a whitish vapour that under certain weather conditions could be seen issuing from the dense trees.

A nicer story tells of the church bell dedicated to St Dunstan, which was said to be a thanks-offering from the local parishioners for deliverance from a great thunderstorm which raged for hours on St Dunstan's Day (May 19th, on a Sunday, though the year is not apparent). So frightened were the villagers, that they hid in their homes until the storm abated, when they perambulated their village with the priest reciting a litany.

BUXTED

IN the 17th century (some say it was later than that) a woman named Nan Tuck, who lived at Rotherfield, poisoned her husband, and when the crime was discovered, fled towards Buxted. As she approached what later became known as Nan Tuck Lane, she remembered the old law of sanctuary, so she started to make for Buxted church. In this she was too late, for her pursuers were almost upon her as she scrambled into Nan Tuck's Wood. There she completely vanished, and hours of searching failed to locate her.

That is one ending to the story. An alternative version is that because she was known as a local witch, the mob was actually chasing her to 'swim' her in the mill pond. (It was believed that a witch would float – innocence could only be proved by drowning.) Her efforts to reach the church were in fact successful, and she was able to grasp the sanctuary ring on the church door. However the vicar pushed her away, saying he could not harbour a witch. She then found her way to Nan Tuck's Wood, where she hanged herself. She was buried without Christian rites, just outside the churchyard wall, and an old stone slab near the lych gate is supposed to cover her burial place.

A pleasanter tale from Buxted is about George Watson, who was nicknamed 'The Calculating Wizard'. Born in 1785, he grew up to be a very simple kind of farm labourer, quite uneducated and without any reading or writing skills. But in spite of this background he could easily perform the most difficult calculations that anyone put to him. Even more astounding, he could recollect the events of every day of his life from an early age. He was taken on tours in Hampshire, Wiltshire, Gloucestershire and Somerset – everywhere astounding all those who saw and talked to him. Eventually he knew every town and village in Sussex and could recall the number of churches and pubs in each.

Mark Anthony Lower (*Contributions to Literature* 1854) said he saw him but once, trudging up Malling Hill, near Lewes, looking considerably the worse for wear, and with his hat chalked all over with figures.

CHALVINGTON

SUSSEX millers have always had a bad press. Most country folk believed that the miller they were forced to deal with (because he was the only one in the immediate neighbourhood) continually cheated them. Honest millers were said to be rare, and to be recognised as one it was necessary to have a tuft of hair growing in the palm of each hand.

Chalvington was supposed to have had such a miller, but his story fails to provide the usual moral, as he was so unsuccessful in business, that he eventually hanged himself. As was the custom with suicides, he was buried at the crossroads, without the benefit of church rites and with an oak stake through his body. The oak grew into a tree, and threw a twisted branch across the road. The whole effect was rather ghostly at night, and before long the spot was considered to be haunted by the ghost of the unfortunate miller.

The more sophisticated locals looked upon the story as a bit of pure folklore, until years later a labourer digging out sand near the roots of the scraggy oak, discovered a human skeleton.

CHANCTONBURY RING

When old Mother Goring's got her cap on,
we shall have some wet.

THIS was an old weather saying, which meant that when Chanctonbury Ring was wearing 'Lady Goring's Night-cap' (cloud) then those below were likely to get rain. The Goring family owned the ring and a good deal of the country around it.

Called 'the Monarch of Sussex Hills', it is one of the most familiar landmarks in the western part of the county, reaching to 700 ft above sea level. From the top, on a clear day, one can see up to 30 miles away, taking in Sussex, Surrey, Hampshire and Kent.

There are many folk tales and legends concerned with the ring. Its origins are said to be due to the Devil when he was digging out a channel into the weald, to allow the sea to swamp the many Sussex churches. His frantic actions threw up sufficient earth to provide Chanctonbury Ring and the Isle of Wight.

On Midsummer Eve (some say May Day Eve, or even any evening) you can raise the Devil by running backwards around the crown of the ring, seven times - but you must run 'widdershins' or anti-clockwise. (At old ceremonies Sussex country folk always processed the opposite way to the sun's course.) The Devil will then offer you a bowl of soup (some say milk) in exchange for your soul. Fairies are said to dwell on the ring and may be seen dancing on Midsummer Eve. There is also a ghost of a mounted man, who gallops past without stopping and then vanishes.

Undoubtedly this most magical place in Sussex is a very eerie spot after nightfall. Many people, over a very long period of time, have had all kinds of uncomfortable feelings when they have tried to stay there all night. Most, it seems, give up after a short time. Even the relatively modern phenomenon of unidentified flying objects, are said to have been sighted there on several occasions.

The top of the ring was undoubtedly used as a Roman temple, and folklore experts have surmised that the ritual of running round 'widdershins' could be a folk-memory of ancient religious dances.

We can be rather more certain about some of the modern history of Chanctonbury Ring, although even that has a legendary feel to it. In 1760 the top was virtually bare of trees, and as a schoolboy, young Charles Goring had the notion of planting a ring of beech trees, to enhance the local landmark. This he did single-handed, toiling up and down the hill with seedlings, and then water. He hardly expected to see the results of his labour, but when he was in his eighties, he was able to write a poem, which included these lines:

Oh! could I live to see the top,
In all its beauty dressed,
That time's arrived; I've had my wish,
And lived to eighty-five.
I'll thank my God who gave such grace,
As long as ere I live.

Charles Goring's trees provided a worthy crown to this monarch of hills, until the horrific night in 1987 when so much of Sussex, including the Chanctonbury beeches, was devastated.

CHICHESTER

IN 1861 William Barrer, the Sussex naturalist, was standing on Pagham Beach, when his eyes rested on the cathedral far away across the fields. He looked out to sea for a moment, then turned to look again at the cathedral and it had disappeared. This was when the cathedral spire fell, and the local rhyme came true:

If Chichester church steeple fall,
In England there's no King at all.

It was of course Queen Victoria who was on the throne of England at that time, so there was no King after all.

Sussex smugglers must have missed the spire, as it was said to be used by them as a landmark for boats approaching from the continent with contraband cargo.

CHIDDINGLY

CHIDDINGLY PLACE, the seat of the Jefferay family, had a legend that a crock of money was kept in a gallery guarded by an evil black hen. The animal was said to sit there night and day without food or drink, guarding the treasure.

A rustic one day decided to make a grab at the crock, but the hen rushed upon him with such fury that he was thrown to the floor, where he lay senseless. The hen then flew out of the great east window, bending two strong iron bars that were in its way. The unfortunate man went out of his mind, and had to be rocked in a cradle like a baby for the rest of his life.

Another tale of Chiddingly Place and the Jefferays relates that they were so proud, they considered the earth too common for them to walk upon. So every Sunday a line of cheeses was laid from their mansion to the church door, for them to step upon. The Jefferay tomb in the church is said to have two of its statues standing upon cheeses.

The monument in the church includes Sir John Jefferay holding a scroll. Tradition says that he dropped down dead with the scroll in his hand, as 'divine judgement on a wicked judge'.

Almost every place in Sussex has its smuggler's story. About a mile from Chiddingly, there was a lane where the smugglers used to meet. One night the government men and the smugglers had a fight there, and several of the latter were killed. Following this, the villagers tried to avoid the lane after dark, because of a ghost which was reputed to walk right through one of the houses.

CISSBURY RING

NEAR Cissbury Ring there is a spot which has the tradition of a phantom highwayman. Because of his crimes he was executed on a gallows by the side of the downland coach road. Before the death sentence was carried out he vowed that he would never sleep in his grave, which was dug in the middle of the road. The morning after his burial, his body was found on top of the grave, and several more attempts to bury him ended with the same result.

Although he eventually stayed put, his ghost on horseback continued to haunt the roadway. A local farmer told how a coach was held up by a highwayman, and deciding to run the thief down, the coach driver urged his horses on, only to find that they and the coach passed through the mounted figure. Carters with their wagons reported that they had bumped over something always at the same spot in the road, although when they looked back there was nothing to be seen.

COWDRAY

THE famed Cowdray House took 60 years to build, but it was all to end in a fire in 1793, when the buildings were left roofless. This, as many will know, was because of a curse – probably the most effective curse ever to have been uttered in Sussex.

The best known version of the legend is that at the dissolution of the monasteries, Battle Abbey was given by Henry VIII to Sir Anthony Browne. The last of the departing monks cursed the new owner, foretelling that his line would perish by fire and water. Sir Anthony Browne's considerable possessions were mainly derived from the spoils of the church, and so it was not surprising that he should be the recipient of such a curse, which was almost a matter of course in such cases. The dreadful words began: 'By the authority of Almighty God and blessed Peter, Prince of the Apostles, to whom it is committed by God the power to bind and loose on earth, let vengeance be declared on the malefactors, robbers, and spoliators of the goods and possessions, rights and liberties, of the Monastery of . . . and of the whole congregation of that monastery, unless they do effectually repent of their malignity.' And much more in similar vein.

Another version is essentially the same except that the speaker is not a monk but the sub-prioress of Easebourne. A third version is that when Sir Anthony was holding his first great feast in the Abbot's Hall at Battle, a monk made his way through the crowd of guests to face Sir Anthony, and uttered the curse, concluding with the words 'By fire and water thy line shall come to an end, and it shall perish out of the land'.

The strangest aspect of the legend is that the curse actually took over 250 years to operate. In 1793 when the great house was gutted by fire, and all its treasures destroyed, the place was empty, and it was thought that a pan of charcoal left burning in the carpenter's workshop had been the cause. At about the same time, the eighth and last Lord Montague, then a young man, was drowned in an ill-judged attempt to negotiate the falls at

Schaffhausen on the Rhine. Storytellers delight in telling of how messengers from England hurried to inform his lordship of the great fire, only to meet other messengers doing the journey in reverse with the news of the young lord's death.

But of course that was not the end of the story. The property passed to Lord Montague's sister, who bore two sons and three daughters. Her husband was out in a boat with the two boys in 1815, when the boat tipped over and the boys were drowned, although he was rescued. Their mother and sisters were watching at the time, and saw it all.

It has been queried that whether, in view of the long period of time before the apparent working of the curse, that perhaps it could be attributed to a chain of coincidences, and that the legend was thought up to fit the events. However, as far back as 1851, a curate at Easebourne wrote that he frequently heard the old villagers tell the story of the curse, and they fully believed that it was a story handed on to them by the servants of the family.

Another Cowdray legend is about the fifth Viscount Montague, who was, according to tradition, a most wicked and violent man. Some versions say that the story began with a dispute between Lord Montague and the priest in the confessional, and the lord killed the priest as he sat in the seat of pardon. Another said that Lord Montague shot the priest at the altar when he dared to begin mass without waiting for the presence of his lordship.

The murderer fled into hiding, whether from the fear of legal retribution or because of his own conscience is not made clear. Whatever the reason he lay concealed for 15 years in a priest's hole in the keeper's lodge, which was said to be only six ft square. It contained an iron chair, and a brass lamp, and could only be reached through a sliding panel in a cupboard in one of the upper bedrooms.

From this dungeon, Lord Montague went out at night into the park, to meet and talk with his wife who remained true to him. She had a habit of wearing a long white dress for these meetings, which may have given rise to the well established tradition of the ghostly white lady of

Cowdray. For many years this part of the grounds was known as 'The Lady's Walk'.

The room in which Lord Montague lived, and died in 1717, was also said to be haunted.

CRAWLEY

ALTHOUGH a post-war 'New Town', Crawley also has a rich and ancient history, and there are many stories and legends concerning the wild nature of the countryside around, and the smugglers and poachers who once frequented the wooded lanes.

The annual spring fair was a great local tradition, held on the 8th of May (said to be the day when all good gardeners planted their runner bean seeds). It was held in the high street until the early 1920s when the volume of traffic caused it to be moved to other sites. (The annual November 5th bonfire had also been held in the high street, but this had been moved ten years earlier.)

This was a poem which managed to bring in almost everything connected with the fair as it was in 1920. It was sold as a broadsheet for one penny:

The Annual Fair on the 8th of May, was larger than has been for many a day.
The Stock in the field fetched a good price, the morning was wet, and cleared off nice.
There were several prime horses, some entire. The rain in the morning made the field in a mire.
A very few pigs, a pen or two of sheep, but nothing in the field was sold very cheap.
From the Middle Square down to 'The Sun', there was plenty of amusement for old and young.
A good lot of horses by 'The George' in the town, which were as usual galloped up to fetch another pound.
There was Houp-la and darts, and swings on the Green, and 'photographs taken' near the pavement was seen.

In the 'White Hart' Field there was plenty going on, two excellent roundabouts belonging to Bond.
A number of swings and coco-nut shying, which were hard to be got with a lot of trying.
Houp-la and darts, and throwing of rings, shooting at bottles and other things.
In Penfold's meadow, near to 'The Sun', was another roundabout, a very good one.
No trying of strength with mallet or Bittle, but other side shows belonging to Whittle.
As you entered the town in the middle square, two or three cheap-jacks were very busy there.
The police were on duty, but things seemed quiet, there was no drunken case, no fighting or riot.
Next day being Sunday, many cleared off soon. Some went home late by the light of the moon.

CROWBOROUGH

THE town was said to be on the main smuggler's route from the coast to East Grinstead. Because it was well wooded and not over populated, it was an excellent place for hiding contraband goods, until the smugglers were ready to move them on. Legend has it that Mead House, which had a number of outbuildings, was one of the most popular places for storing the illicit goods.

A headless ghost of one of the smugglers was reputed to haunt a local hill, where he carried a lantern, forever searching for the place where he had hidden his cache of smuggled spirits.

Another most unusual ghost was associated with this area. In Jarvis Brook Road, several people claimed to have seen a spectre in the form of a bag of soot. A blacksmith who saw it one night took courage and defied it to do its worst, but when it started to chase him, he took fright and ran for home pursued by the black bag.

There were also witches. Dame Neve was suspected of bewitching a butter churn. (Many dairywomen whose butter refused to 'come', must have felt that witchery was at work.) In this particular instance, help was at hand, as someone suggested putting a hot poker into the churn (witches are said to be afraid of iron). Of course Dame Neve was discovered soon afterwards with a bad burn on her leg.

Time and time again the old story crops up of a witch turning herself at will into a hare. It is a very old belief, and recurs all over Europe. Another of Crowborough's witches, Dame Garson, was supposed to have the ability to change into a hare. On one occasion when the hare was chased by a pack of hounds, it leaped through her cottage window, and the huntsmen heard her voice exclaiming 'Ah, my boys, you ain't got me yet'.

CUCKFIELD

MANY ghosts have an annoying similarity, which can make the stories about them seem rather boring and monotonous. Not so Geranium Jane of the Kings Head at Cuckfield. She was said to be a young girl who was having an affair with the licensee, at an unknown time during the 19th century. After a lover's quarrel, he killed her with a flower pot containing geraniums. She was buried in the churchyard not far away, but had a habit of returning as a ghost always accompanied by a strong smell of the flowers which killed her. She is supposed to have been seen in fairly modern times, and dogs are said to growl and raise their hackles when she appears. It has been suggested that having geranium plants within the inn is a sure way to run the risk of the ghost making an appearance. Once these particular flowers are banished, she stays away.

Giants have always exerted a fascination and apart from the really legendary ones, others actually existed and became part of continuing legends. Such a one was Henry Blacker, known as 'The Cuckfield Giant', who was born in

1724. He was 7 ft 4 in tall, and was brought up to labour on a farm, like most of the other village boys. In his twenties he realised the possibilities offered by his unusual stature, and encouraged by the Duke of Cumberland, he began to exhibit himself at fairs and other events throughout Sussex. When he was 27, he was shown in London as 'The British Giant'. No doubt this paid better than working in the fields, but there seems no record of how long he lived, or indeed how he spent the rest of his life.

DITCHLING

A WITCH who lived in a cottage in Ditchling had the unusual nickname of 'Jack o' Spades'. Like many other witches she had the power to stop the carters with their wagons, or let them move when she wished. She is said to have gone out one night in the form of a hare, and was chased by men with dogs who had been waiting for such an opportunity. As always seemed to happen, she escaped in the nick of time, by jumping through her cottage window, sustaining a nip from one of the hounds as she did so. The next morning she sent for a neighbour to come in and put a plaster on a wound which had mysteriously appeared on her leg.

Whether this particular witch had anything to do with them is not clear, but there was a persistent legend concerning the Downs near Ditchling Beacon, which told of the 'witch hounds' which could be heard yelping as they raced through the night. Sometimes they were accompanied by hoof beats and the call of the hunting horn. Esther Meynell speaks of them being heard as late as 1935. They may be compared with the 'wish hounds' of Dartmoor or the 'gabriel hounds' of Durham.

DUNCTON

TUNNELS and passages always fascinate, and are invariably linked by legend with their use by smugglers, or perhaps priests during times of religious persecution.

From a newspaper report in 1986 it is interesting to hear of substantial tunnels being discovered, apparently for the first time since they were actually in use. They are at Bigenor Farm, Duncton; the present buildings dating from 1797. Two beautifully arched tunnels under one side of the house lead to a cellar. In the cellar is a fireplace with a tiny entrance through the back. This leads into a 4 ft high underground passage, which is 40 ft long and ends near the river Rother. Although the true reason for the tunnels is not known, local tradition speaks of smugglers.

EASTDEAN

BEFORE the erection of the Beachy Head lighthouse in 1831, Jonathan Darby, vicar of Eastdean from 1706 to 1718 (some accounts give different dates), excavated a cavern and staircase at the base of Belle-Toute, which became known as 'Parson Darby's Hole'.

Until the late 19th century, this was the only refuge for shipwrecked crews, and consisted of two apartments, big enough to contain a group of sailors or other travellers. The project was entirely his own work, and he went there on stormy nights, hanging out a great lamp to attract the attention of any who needed help.

Tradition says that he once preserved twelve Dutch sailors in this way, and on another occasion the crew of a brig with 23 hands. He was remembered in Eastdean after his death, as a sturdy old man in knee breeches and beaver hat, riding to hounds. One cottager had acquired his clock, and exhibited it proudly.

The cave remained until at least 1904 but at some time after that it was washed away. A correspondent in the

Sussex County Magazine in 1944 said that there was no trace of it by that time.

It all makes a wonderful story, but there are some dissenting voices. A local legend says that the caves were there long before Darby's time, and had been used by smugglers. This seems possible, but of course he may have found them, perhaps enlarged them, and put them to far better use.

Another local story is that he was driven on certain nights to the caves, not so much to watch for distressed sailors, as to get away from the rough temper of his wife. She died in 1723, and he survived until 1728, succumbing to exposure from cold and damp. When his wife died he was said to be desolate, and their joint gravestone speaks of 'My beloved Anne', so it appears that the stories about her were, to say the least, exaggerated.

EAST GRINSTEAD

MANY stories are told about the famous hymn writer, Dr John Mason Neale. Here is a little ghost story in which he features. One day when he was crossing the quadrangle of Sackville College, the beautiful group of almshouses of which he was warden, the ghost of a lady friend who had recently died appeared to him. She implored him to save her husband from committing a crime he was contemplating. Neale went to the husband, and as a friend tried to persuade him not to proceed with the felony. It was only by describing the apparition in detail, that he was able to persuade the man that it was his wife's wish that he should desist.

EAST HOATHLY

THE most infamous Sussex cannibal lived at Brede, but he was not the only one. At East Hoathly, the Cavalier colonel, Sir Thomas Lunsford, one of twins, was said to dine upon children. He had a bad time in 1632 when he was tried for killing deer, and a murderous assault in the park of Sir Thomas Pelham. He took a pot shot at Sir Thomas, but escaped with a fine. In 1649 he emigrated from East Hoathly to Virginia in the USA. His earlier reputation as a child eater may have had something to do with the Roundheads, who claimed that when he was wounded in battle, a child's limb was seen protruding from his pocket. A Roundhead rhyme of the time ended with the line 'From Lunsford deliver us, that eateth up children'. A ballad of the same period was even more explicit, with the words 'He swore he saw, when Lunsford fell, a child's arm in his pocket'. Not the only time that adversaries in war have credited their opponents with unspeakable crimes!

A relatively modern commentary on the old legend was provided in 1935, by a correspondent in the *Sussex County Magazine* who told how as a child (in the 1860s) he was frequently reminded that if he went near the river or canal, 'Bloody Bones' who lived under the bank, would grab him with his blood-stained hands.

EAST PRESTON

THERE is a well remembered tradition that when the windmill (presumably Miller Oliver's post mill) on Highdown Hill blew down, a millstone was unseated and rolled on its edge down to the road leading to the bottom of Highdown. At this point versions of the story differ. Some say that a farm labourer on the road was struck by the stone and killed, being found the following morning trapped under the stone. There are even slight variations on this story, but basically such an accident seems possible.

Another version has it that the millstone continued rolling as far as the crossroads (now beneath the railway crossing) ending up on a suicide's grave. I am assured that this would be quite impossible. Another twist to the story is that the millstone was placed upon the body of a suicide, with a stake through the centre, to prevent the ghost haunting the neighbourhood. A correspondent to a local Sussex newspaper spoke of a number of millstones which once rested against a nearby wall.

ETCHINGHAM

THE interesting 14th century Church of The Assumption and St. Nicholas, once had a bell which was lost in the moat, which at one time surrounded the church. The usual Sussex bell legend says that it can never be recovered except with the help of six white oxen. Certainly the area around the church is said to be very wet, but apart from this there are no other details to add to the legend.

FITTLEWORTH

MRS Charlotte Latham writing in 1868 told of the legend of the puck bird, or puck. This was supposed to be another name for the Devil, although the word also has fairy connections. It was believed to be a mischievous spirit which inflicted on calves and heifers a mysterious disease called the puck complaint or the puckeridge. When the puck bird decides to descend on cattle it is an object of terror to the superstitious, as it springs up suddenly, unlike more normal birds.

At Fittleworth a servant sent upon an errand was overlong in returning. When chided for this, she gave as a good reason for her delay, that the puck bird had flown in front of her and she dare not overtake it.

There are many legends in Sussex of snakes or serpents, so large that they were referred to as dragons. Such a beast was supposed to have terrified the good folk of Fittleworth during the 1860s. It was described in Sussex dialect as 'oudaciously large'. Its lair was near a pathway, and it would not allow anyone to pass, rushing out with a terrible hissing and a very bad smell, to drive back the unfortunate person who had dared to go near it.

As in so many Sussex villages, Fittleworth had its wise woman (a sort of white witch) who would be sent for whenever one of her neighbours was suffering from any minor hurt. She would bow her head over a burn, crossing two fingers over it, and then recite the following:

There came two angels from the North,
One was fire and one was frost.
Out fire, in frost,
In the name of the Father, Son and Holy Ghost.

This was one of several well known folk charms which were widely used up to about 100 years ago in Sussex. They were sometimes sold written out on scraps of paper, at fairs. The seller would ask but a few pence for the charm, and sometimes the recipient would not even be able to read the words – but would still treasure the charm.

The wise woman, after saying the words, would breathe quickly on the wound. Presumably the burn eventually got better, and the reputation of the white witch, and her charms, was further enhanced.

Another Fittleworth lady, at about the same time, kept a small dame school. She was a celebrated compounder of ointments, and was also said to be a charmer of wounds caused by thorns. Her charm ran as follows:

Our Saviour Christ was of a pure virgin born,
And he was crowned with a thorn,
I hope it may not rage or swell,
I trust in God it will do well.

The same lady confessed that she had inherited from her mother a charm for the bite of a viper, and another that cured giddiness in cattle. She never made any charge for her charms, so she was evidently in much demand with patients who had not the money to pay for the doctor's conventional cures.

Some of her charms had been taught to her as a young girl just going out to service, by an old shepherd, who lodged with her mother. When she treated a lad who had been stung by a viper coiled up in a bird's nest, she found him with a swollen arm 'as big as her body'. She waited until she could get him by himself, recited the blessing over his arm 'and he was soon quite hearty again'. Since he had grown up, he had many times been to see her, saying that she was the best friend he had ever had. A farmer too, came to her from a distance, begging her to save his cow that had been taken ill suddenly. She said her charm, without even seeing the animal, and by the time the farmer got home the cow was completely well.

Mrs Latham said that when she tried to obtain further charms from one of the Fittleworth wise women, she was told 'I promised the man who taught them to me, by all that's good and great, never to tell them to any one; but I did not say I would not write them down, and I have done so, and they will be found after my death, for I should like to know I have done some good to my neighbours after I am gone.'

Obviously these folk charms and blessings had a very great hold upon the superstitious minds of most of the country people. The strange mixture of Christianity and paganism within them, shows how much the two beliefs were still alive in the peasant mind.

GORING – BY – SEA

WHEN Goring-by-Sea was still a village, and not just part of Worthing, it was united to its larger neighbour by a lane bordered by high hedges and tall elms. On the north side, well in Goring, was a barn from which seemed to emanate an evil influence that terrified every passing horse.

Horses passing this barn would always swerve to the opposite side of the road, and sometimes would not proceed at all. It was then necessary to turn back to Worthing, and reach home by a very roundabout route, making a journey of three or four miles.

Today the barn has disappeared, and the lane has become a wide road, so presumably the evil spirit has been well and truly exorcised.

GRAFFHAM

WHEN Mr Burgess took up his new appointment as the minister at Graffham, he was returning late one night from an appointment in London. At the outskirts of the parish, he became very apprehensive because of the great darkness of the night, and the many ditches thereabouts, which were unfamiliar to him. He went on his knees and begged God to guide him safely to his new home, whereupon a light shone around him and accompanied him closely till he arrived safely at his house. We are told that he was a sober and honest man, not given to flights of fancy.

The local witch was Old Mother Pratt. The local children taunted her with:

Granny Pratt, caught a rat,
Stuck it in her Sunday Hat.

According to a local man she is supposed to have bewitched a neighbour's pony in its field, so that it couldn't be made to move. On another occasion a cart stuck on the hill near to her cottage, and the carter was unable to make it move. He struck at the wheel with a piece of metal, and a hare ran out straight into her cottage.

When this happened a second time, dogs were let loose. The hare darted up a drain pipe outside the witch's cottage, but one of the hounds caught it by the leg and drew blood. Mother Pratt was later found upstairs in her bed, with blood flowing out under the bedclothes. It is worth noting that hares have always been considered magical animals, and that if one was seen as the first animal when leaving home, then the journey might as well be abandoned until another day.

At Lavington House, Garton Orme was the wicked squire in the early 18th century. He was a gambler, a womaniser and had many other bad habits. His wife, who opposed his wicked ways, mysteriously disappeared. He announced that she was suffering from an infectious disease, and would allow none of the servants near her room. He then said that the illness had proved fatal, and a coffin was taken to the church and hurriedly interred. But many of the village people had other ideas, and it was even rumoured that Garton had pushed his wife down a disused well on the estate.

He then proceeded to marry the rector's daughter Anne, who came with a good dowry. This helped his money problems, but it did not stop his affair with a local lady called Joan Goble. She gave birth to a baby, and her father, Hezekiah Goble, vowed vengeance. He stood under a willow tree and cursed the evil man who had ruined his daughter, vowing that no male heir should be given to him or his successors.

Garton Orme died in 1758, and was buried in Lavington churchyard, and his death was followed by stories of hauntings. The curse also appeared to work; so much so that a lord of the manor in the 19th century sought to exorcise it by solemnly burning the willow tree under which Hezekiah had stood.

But what of the story of the wife and the disused well? In 1845 some coffins were moved in the church during rebuilding. One struck the workmen as being unusually heavy, and permission was given for it to be opened. It was found to contain – just stones!

HAILSHAM

A LARGE stone called the Amberstone lies on the northern boundary of the parish. Local tradition has it that at every full moon, and every time the church clock strikes midnight, the stone turns round on its bed.

A story (with a lot more point to it), is told by Thomas Geering in his book *Our Sussex Parish* (1884). A young woman believed implicitly in charms, ghosts and tokens. To choose her husband, she used an oracle. This was a basin of cold spring water, in which were dropped three separate slips of paper, wrapped in balls of paste made of wheaten flour. On each slip were the initial letters of three possible husbands. The first to rise to the top of the water bore the initials JH, so he was the chosen one.

After 50 years of happily married life, she was able to report 'What the Gods did for us, they did well'. They were buried as they had lived, close together, under one mound in the old churchyard. Well, that's the story!

HARTFIELD

HARTFIELD provides us with a charming story, concerning a wealthy man in the early 17th century, who determined to find out the true nature of his Sussex countrymen. His name was Nicholas Smith, nicknamed 'Beggarman Smith', for he travelled around the Sussex villages, disguised as a beggar, asking for food and alms. It seems that little Hartfield was the first place where he was received with any real kindness. He settled at

Crotchford Manor, and in his will of October 18th 1634 left £10 to be shared in perpetuity between 40 poor people.

'Beggarman' is still honoured every Good Friday, when a short service is held by his grave, with the rector and the churchwardens. The income for the continuance of the charity now comes from investments held by the Charity Commissioners, and implemented by other grants.

Some accounts of 'Beggarman Smith' confuse him with Henry Smith, a Surrey man, who held much land in Sussex. He died in 1627, leaving much of his money and possessions to charity. He was almost always accompanied in life by a dog, so his nickname was fittingly 'Dog Smith'.

HARTING

IT has been said that Harting was once a hot bed of superstition; certainly it is a charming village, which thrives on tradition.

In 1727 Timothy Luff was buried in the churchyard. He claimed to be a wizard or sorcerer, with mesmeric powers, who could cast horoscopes. (The title wizard is unusual in Sussex, as both males and females with magic powers are usually termed witches.)

A fortune teller (was it Timothy Luff?) was ejected from East Harting House, and according to tradition, caused hot flints to rain down on the village from the Downs.

The local witch was Old Mother Digby, who lived in Hogs Lane. Like all the other self-respecting Sussex witches, she was capable of turning herself into a hare at will. Squire Russell, when out hunting with his hounds, always lost the hare near a drain outside the old lady's house. One day the dogs caught the hare by its hind-quarters, as it escaped down the drain. The Squire, opening the old dame's door, found her rubbing exactly the same part of her body. Does this story sound familiar?

One last claim to fame for Harting – Emma Stanley,

who was described as 'the Queen of the gypsies' was supposed to have been buried in Harting churchyard in 1848.

HASTINGS

THIS East Sussex coastal town, with an 'old town' alongside more modern developments, is rich in folklore and legends.

About the year 1694 the people of Hastings were in great poverty, in fact many were starving to death. God sent an unusually great shoal of herrings up the river; enough to supply the inhabitants for a week. Seven days later another great shoal of cod appeared, again supplying the people with all their needs. A nice legend, but we are not told what they did when the cod ran out.

As recently as 1830 there lived near the Rope Walk, a repulsive old woman who local people claimed was a witch. She went about bent almost double, supporting herself with a crutch. Undoubtedly she encouraged the popular idea of her evil powers, by wearing a bright red cloak, and positively delighting in the idea that, old and miserable as she was, she was powerful enough to strike awe into the hearts of other folk.

Timid people crouched out of sight at her approach, and most others went out of their way to avoid her if they could. A girl living nearby was afflicted with lameness, and her mother was convinced that the old witch was responsible for her daughter's condition.

It was universally believed that she could assume the form of a cat, and many a harmless puss was hunted to death by boys who convinced themselves that they were chasing the witch in her feline guise.

Also in the 19th century, there lived in Hastings a fisherman who, it was said, had sold himself to the Devil. It was believed that the man could enter a house through a keyhole and that he had even encouraged his daughter to become a witch. Another of his tricks was to sit on the points of pins without feeling pain. Some of his brother fishermen tried to test out this claim, and accordingly they placed a number of long and sharp needles in the cushion on his chair. Sure enough, when he sat down he never even flinched.

The ruins of the castle are supposed to be haunted by at least two ghosts. The first is a nun in a brown habit, who has been seen digging. The popular idea is that she was put to death for breaking her vows. A caretaker and his wife are supposed to have seen her quite regularly, and her image is also said to have been captured on film taken by a visitor to the castle precincts. At one period a London medium is said to have gone into a trance, and made contact with the nun.

Another castle ghost is a middle-aged woman in a brown dress of Victorian style. Holding a baby in her arms, she moves towards the cliff edge and then vanishes. Legend says that she committed suicide by jumping from the cliff, after she bore an illegitimate child by a local fisherman, who callously rejected her.

Below the castle are the famous St Clement's Caves, taking up around three acres. These are said to be of natural formation, much enlarged by human hands. Legends prefer to attribute them variously to the Romans, the Danes, smugglers, or even that they were hollowed out to serve as dungeons for the castle. A man digging the foundations for his greenhouse in 1825 claimed to have discovered them, although they were certainly known long before that date. There is a feature in the caves called a font, although its purpose is not clear. There is also a very large open space known as 'The Ballroom', and in fact has been so used. One passage is known as 'The Whispering Gallery'. Many supernatural stories have been woven around the caves, and the carved figures which they contain. One is said to be of St Clement, or some other religious figure, others may be Harold, Napoleon, the Duke of Wellington, or even just a common smuggler. We can be sure that members of the latter fraternity must have found the caves very useful at times.

In Hastings 'Old Town' there is a tiny house popularly known as 'The Piece of Cheese' on account of its shape. Said to have been built in 1871 as a bet, it occupies a small triangle of land 30 ft x 24 ft x 17 ft. It is claimed to be the second smallest house in Britain, and the only three-cornered house in the world.

Lastly a much fuller, and in the main, nicer legend than most. This story is about 'The Lover's Seat, at Fairlight Glen, Hastings. Like all good legends, there are several versions. Not in doubt is the year 1786, when a young sailor, Charles Lamb, of a well known Rye family, was commanding the revenue cutter *The Stag,* which was engaged in hunting smugglers. (Amazing how smugglers manage to get into so many Sussex legends.) He was in love with 19 year old Elizabeth, the only child and heiress of Mr Boys of Elford, near Hawkhurst who was sometimes called 'The Squire of Fairlight'. Mr Boys was violently opposed to the match of his daughter with the young sailor, and to prevent her seeing him he placed her in a house near the glen, in the charge of a trusted servant. Almost needless to say, the pair still managed to meet, and the girl was even able to signal to her lover's ship from the top of the cliff. In some accounts, young Charles is actually said to have been able to climb the cliff in order to meet his Elizabeth.

This is where the different versions of the tale take over. What seems certain is that the lovers eloped and were married, although some say that it was at St Clement Dane's church, in the Strand, London, whereas others would have us believe that the marriage took place in Hollington Church-in-the-Wood. The father did not forgive them, but the brave sailor built a house for his bride at Salehurst and they lived there happily for 28 years, until he was sadly drowned in Southampton Water. The couple's daughter married a Mr Ferris, and they had many Sussex descendants.

At least that is one ending. The alternative, which was much more popular with story-tellers and ballad sellers, was that the girl was unable to get away to marry her lover, and in desperation threw herself from the cliff top crying 'The shells of the ocean shall be my bed, and the shrimps go wagging over my head'. Even from here the story can take two directions. One is that her clothes caught on a tree, the sailor saw his love through his telescope, and was able to rescue her. The other is that she was drowned – or even that they were both drowned. Hence a popular name for the beauty spot 'Lover's Leap'. The second versions were obviously much more popular, having all the attributes of a typical Victorian tear-jerker.

What we are now sure of is that the spot is a perfect sun trap even on a winter's day, and is still enjoyed by young lovers. For a long while there has been a seat here, although it was hurled into the sea by a soldier in the war – but happily replaced. Those who have sampled the delights of the seat will, I feel sure, prefer to believe in the first version of the legend.

HAYWARDS HEATH

SUSSEX history often told of huge snake or dragon-like creatures that were seen in the forests, and sometimes killed by local people, who never stopped talking about it afterwards.

In 1794 at Haywards Heath, one of these huge snakes was shot. It was said to be nearly 5 ft long, and proportionately large in every other way. Locals said they had seen it many times before, but it always disappeared under the earth when approached.

HEATHFIELD

CADE Street is said to be named after the rebel Jack Cade who was killed here in 1450 by Alexander Iden, Sheriff of Kent. The event is commemorated by a stone pillar.

The historical account says that after an initial victory over the Royal forces at Sevenoaks the rebels entered London and were repulsed with great slaughter. On receiving a promise of pardon, they dispersed. The rebel Cade was chased by Iden and his men from Kent, and it was in Heathfield that they caught up with him. Cade hid in a garden, but was found and taken prisoner after a struggle in which he was badly wounded, dying on his way to London in a cart.

There are several legends surrounding Cade's death. One story says that Cade invaded Iden's garden, and when discovered attacked Iden – although Iden said that he did not know who he was at the time. Another version says that Cade was playing bowls in the inn garden, when Iden, recognising him, killed him with an arrow.

Any account of Heathfield legends and tales would not be complete without a reference to the 'Hefful Cuckoo Fair' ('Hefful' was the old name for Heathfield). This was held each year on the 14th April, when folklore said that the old lady let the first cuckoo out of her basket. Depending on what kind of a mood she was in, she might allow more than just one to escape. Actually, the first cuckoo in Sussex is often heard before the 14th. The old rhyme goes:

In March in vain for him you'll search,
In April he shows his bill,
In May he sings both night and day,
In June he changes his tune,
In July away he flies
In August away he must,
And if you hear him in September,
Tis as late as the oldest man can remember.

In 1868 a woman of the village complained of the bad humour of the cuckoo-keeper, who had only let one bird fly out of her apron, and 'that 'ere bird is nothing to call a singer'. A well known belief in Heathfield and elsewhere in Sussex is that when the cuckoo is first heard, you should turn the money over in your pocket. If you haven't any money, or neglect to turn it over, then you will be poor for the rest of the year.

HELLINGLY

HERE is Horselunges Manor, a 15th century timber house, which is supposed to have the ghost of John Busbrig, who died there in 1547 whilst fighting off a gang of poachers.

Another story is of Agnes Devenish, who in 1491 managed to get a stone stuck in her nose, which resulted in an abscess and fever which threatened her life. Her distracted mother cried for help to the spirit of Henry IV, and the stone miraculously fell out, saving the child's life.

HENFIELD

HENFIELD once had a ghost in the form of an animal the size of a calf, with flaming eyes. It was seen several times in a wood much frequented by smugglers. There is another legend of a headless lady, who was said to sit and spin on Pickwell Bridge. Like many Sussex ghosts these could have been smugglers' inventions, designed to frighten the more law-abiding folk away from the areas which they used regularly. It is noticeable that smugglers' ghosts are often headless – this was probably considered the ultimate in horror.

On All-Hallows Day (November 1st) over 300 years ago, a charity was instituted in Henfield which is still carried out annually. This is Dame Gresham's Charity, which began in 1661 when this good lady, who was a member of the well known local family of Byshopp, left in her will instructions that ten shillings should be devoted annually to a sermon in the parish church, and that the remaining profits from a field of seven acres should be used to clothe some of the poorer folk of Henfield. To the original field, sometimes known as Flannel Field, was added later in 1705 a second field.

The charity has been carried on with very little change. Between the wars various items of clothing were distributed, including flannel. During the Second World

War clothing vouchers which could be used in the town of Henfield were substituted. Today the income comes mainly from the rent received from the two fields, and also a small amount from an investment made through the charity commissioners. Originally the charity was distributed each year in the church, then in the Old Coffee Tavern or the Assembly Rooms. In more modern times the ceremony has been taken back into the church.

HIGHDOWN HILL

HIGHDOWN Hill, close to Worthing, is a splendid open space, much loved by walkers and nature lovers. For many years it has been well known as the site of 'The Miller's Tomb'. Miller Oliver, unlike many other Sussex millers, was a local favourite, in spite of (or perhaps because of) his many eccentricities. He was born in 1709, and was particularly noted for having erected his own tomb, inscribed with verses and other inscriptions, 30 years prior to his death when he was 84. The tomb, which was badly damaged in 1982, but subsequently rebuilt, was close to his mill, which was demolished in 1826. It occupies a favoured spot with visitors, and has been a local landmark for a very long time. Local children know it well, and Winifred Whiting told me that when she was young, the youngsters believed that the inscription on the tomb stated that anyone who ran round it twelve times at midnight, would make the Devil jump out of the tomb and give chase. Of course it said no such thing, but in fact this story or variants of it, have been around a long time. Sometimes the number is given as the magical seven; the perambulation around the tomb must be undertaken backwards; or it would be the ghost of the miller himself who would appear, rather than the Devil. Circling some object seven times in order to raise a ghost, or the evil one, is a very old and well known folk belief, found in many places.

Miller Oliver, although not, as far as we can make out,

a melancholy man, seems to have been a trifle obsessed with his eventual end. He made his own coffin and kept it under his bed, fitting castors to it so that he could pull it out easily each night to check it over. One of his many interests was in writing poetry, and on the coffin he is said to have written:

Beneath my bed my coffin stands,
On four wheels swift it runs.

At his funeral there were a number of young maidens, all in white, one of which read a sermon over his grave – some said written by himself, although this was apparently not so. Over 2,000 people are supposed to have been present at the interment but this was probably an exaggeration. A legend exists that he was buried upside-down in the tomb, so that at the day of judgement when the world is turned upside-down, he would be the only one to be the right way up. A similar tale has been told of other eccentrics.

Another side to his character was his ability as a smuggler, not an uncommon secondary trade at that time, and one not likely to have affected his popularity. The path from the sea to Highdown Hill was once known as 'Smugglers Walk', and no doubt his mill on the hill provided an excellent look-out point.

He was also an amateur craftsman and delighted in mechanical models, two of which adorned the top of his dwelling. One was of a miller filling a sack, and the other was equally appropriate, as it was of a customs officer chasing a smuggler, and behind him an old woman laying into him with her broom. Children loved them, but unfortunately I do not think they have survived.

The site has even more ancient history, as a large Saxon burial ground was unearthed in the 1800s, and over 80 skeletons and many other artifacts were discovered. In the mid 19th century, an old woman, Hannah White, sold home made sweets to the visitors, and with a little financial encouragement would tell a much elaborated story of the miller and his tomb.

HOLLINGTON

LAMB wrote about St Leonard's church at Hollington describing it as: 'A little churchling in the midst of a wood that seems dropped by an angel that was tired of carrying two packages'. Certainly it is unusual to find a church in the midst of a wood, although perhaps when the Sussex weald was much more wooded than it is today, this was not so. The legend is that when work was begun on the little 'Church-in-the-Wood', the Devil undid all the work that was done each day, as he claimed the site as his own. Priests were summoned to exorcise the evil one's influence, but as they began their prayers a voice was heard saying that all opposition would cease if the building spot was changed. The builders must have been realists, because they accepted at once, and the church was built some distance away. The sequel is that a thick wood grew up around it, but whether as a bit of revenge from the satanic one, or as protection from his influence, is not clear.

HORAM

THE builders of a church at Horam were less persistent than some others, as when their work on a field at Horeham Farm (called Church Field) was removed each night by supernatural forces, they gave up and the church was not finished – in fact a church was not built here until 1890. A rare instance of presumably evil forces triumphing over the simple but obstinate Sussex folk.

HORSHAM

LIKE most old Sussex towns, Horsham has many tales of the supernatural and the unexplained. Writing in 1868 Lady Hurst referred to Chesworth House and its tales of ghostly bells and shrieks, and the bloodstains on the stones which no amount of cleaning would remove, culminating with the stones having to be completely taken up. At midnight, so it was said, warriors on horseback can be seen rushing down the neighbouring hill. Now these stories are little spoken about, and we can only assume that the ghosts have been exorcised.

Knepp Castle, near Horsham, had the ghost of a white doe, which was supposed to be the spirit of a young girl who had been bewitched in the 13th century.

Probably Horsham's best known ghost is Squire Powlett (whose tomb is in West Grinstead church). He was said to leap on the back of your horse, if you were unwise enough to venture into the depths of St Leonard's Forest at night. The forest has many other legends, which have been dealt with fully elsewhere; sufficient to point out that as well as ghosts, it was also the haunt of smugglers, so it has to be admitted that where there was one there was usually the other. In fact I have heard it said that when smugglers grew too old to take part in the actual work, they drew a kind of pension in return for donning white sheets at night, and playing the parts of respectable ghosts.

Strangely enough the story of the headless ghost of Squire Powlett is still told today, and I have even had an account given to me by a lady who described how her husband saw a headless phantom on the side of one of the hammer ponds in the forest in very recent times. I was also told of how in 1977 a group of senior boys from a Horsham school asked permission to spend a night in St Leonard's Forest, with cameras, trip wire and other technical equipment. At one minute to midnight they were so disturbed by unearthly noises that they left in a very great hurry. It was three days before they gained enough nerve to return to the spot, and retrieve their cameras etc.

Another well known Horsham story, which always

causes a shudder when it is told, is about the last time that pressing to death as a legal execution was carried out in this country. This was in Horsham gaol in 1735, following the trial of John Weekes of Fittleworth (known as 'The Dumb Man') for the murder of Elizabeth Symonds. He had three accomplices; one turned King's Evidence, and the other two were convicted and hanged. John Weekes refused to plead, making out that he was completely dumb, although eight witnesses swore that they had heard him speak before the trial. He was taken to Horsham, where in the prison yard before a large crowd of onlookers, he was ceremoniously crushed to death by large weights of iron and stone being placed on him. To deliver the final act, it was said that the executioner had to jump on to the pile to add his own weight.

The sequel is that when the executioner was taking the body of the unfortunate John Weekes to the burial place for felons in Horsham churchyard (known as Hell Corner), the body fell out of the barrow at the Kings Head corner. He replaced it, and carried on, but fell down dead at exactly the same spot a few days later. At least that is one version, another is that when he was carrying the body of the executed man to the burial place, he noticed a light in the Crown (another Horsham inn). The porter, who was a friend of his, called him in for a drink, and the executioner turned the body out of the barrow and hid it behind a gate. After he had finished drinking, he replaced the body and carried on. The end was the same – he fell down dead at that spot a few days later.

One of the oldest parts of Horsham is the Causeway, the attractive tree-lined road leading to the parish church. Not surprisingly this has been mentioned in several Horsham ghost stories. On more than one occasion a figure of what appears to be a monk has been seen at the north end of the churchyard. There is a very old house on this corner, and the ghost has been seen from there, although not actually by the lady who was in residence at the time, but by a visitor. In the 1940s the monk was seen by the vicar, disappearing close to the vicarage. I have visited a house halfway along the Causeway which the owner claimed had a resident ghost. She was quite unafraid, and even had a name for him. He appeared to spend most time in one particular room or the staircase leading to it. She told me how the temperature appeared to drop just within this one room at certain times. At the town end of the Causeway there is the seemingly old Town Hall, although this is not as ancient as it looks. There are several tales of ghosts having been heard and seen here by people who have been alone in the building late at night. There are also stories of ghosts in Cambridge Road, Kings Road and in an old cottage near Roffey Corner.

My mother and my aunts used to make my blood chill with stories of a house behind the old Catholic church in Springfield Road. Their recollections were of strange noises, and poltergeist activity when the house was used by the young people of the parish as a youth club. This got so bad, that the club room had to be closed. The late Canon Walter Stone told me rather more of the story, which apparently started in 1879 when Father Munro was the parish priest, and actually lived in the house. One of the manifestations which he experienced regularly was of a crucifix which hung in the hall, falling from its nail. There was rapping on the walls, and footsteps in the upper rooms. A dog owned by the housekeeper would bristle and stand staring at something which was not apparent to anyone else. The front door bell and other bells in the house would ring constantly without human aid. The priest thought this might be caused by rats, and so he fastened up the bell wires but without effect. Then he thought about boys playing tricks (ring and run) and called in the aid of the Police. One night he thought he had caught the culprit, and so did the policeman. Father Munro opened the front door quickly, and caught the policeman who was creeping along outside with the same idea in mind.

Canon Langton George Vere, who was a friend of Father Munro, verified these happenings by his own experiences when visiting the presbytery, and he wrote it up in fictionalised form as a story in a book published in 1897. Apparently the present day presbytery on the opposite side of the road, was the result of these strange manifestations. Father Munro's health was so obviously affected that when he related the story to the Duke of Norfolk, the Duke had the new presbytery built.

Folklore did not die at the end of the 19th century, it still exists although not always recognised as such. Nowadays people talk about 'urban folk tales', and these – often with a very macabre theme, are found all over the country. An example is the 'phantom hitch hiker' which in different forms is one of the most common. One of these stories has been located in Horsham. (The following account is in Jacqueline Simpson's book *The Folklore of Sussex,* published in 1973, although other versions exist.) A motorist gave a lift to a girl who was hitching southwards on the London-Worthing road. As he passed through Horsham, he felt like a cup of coffee, so he stopped at a cafe. The girl refused to get out, so he left her sitting in the car. When he returned she had gone and no one could tell him what had happened to her. Worried by this he phoned her parents (she had mentioned her address to him). To his horror he learnt that their only daughter had been killed three years before, run over whilst hitching a lift outside a Horsham cafe.

Somewhat akin to these modern folk stories, are the many accounts of big cats or pumas, which crop up from time to time, mainly in Surrey, but also in Sussex. In March 1975 two girls horse riding were thrown from their mounts, when a 'big cat' crossed their path. Two days later there was a report of a somewhat similar beast being sighted at Pease Pottage, near Horsham, sitting near the end of the M23.

In the period 1559 to 1701 18 women were indicted for witchcraft in Sussex, although of these only four were found guilty and only one hanged. This was Margaret Cooper of Kirdford who was executed in Horsham, having been found guily of bewitching three people so that they died. The last Sussex trial for witchcraft was in Horsham in 1680 when Alice Nash was charged with bewitching Elizabeth Slater age 2½, and her sister Anne Slater. She was found not guilty and acquitted. All witchcraft laws were repealed in 1736, although this did not mean that people stopped believing in witches. However it must be said that Sussex, including Horsham, was not nearly as harsh in its treatment of witches as some other parts of the country. No witches were burnt in Sussex, contrary to what many people believe, although

Ann Whale and Ann Cruttenden were burnt at the stake for murder, being dragged on a hurdle to Broadbridge Heath Common for the barbaric sentence to be carried out.

HOVE

IN Hove Park you can see the Goldstone, a large piece of stone measuring 13ft 6in long, 9ft high, and 5ft 6in at its greatest thickness. The story of the stone is that in 1833 Farmer Rigden was annoyed at having it on his land, either because of the visitors who came to view it, or perhaps merely because it stopped him utilising one of his fields efficiently. A hole 16ft deep was excavated and the stone was buried. In 1900, after having been buried for 67 years it was dug up and relocated to Hove Park, where it was surrounded by other smaller stones from a different site in Goldstone Bottom. The stone has always been associated with much folklore. The best known legend is that it was thrown to its original position at Goldstone Farm by the Devil when he was excavating at the Devils Dyke, to drown the wealden churches. Other legends stem from the belief that the stone has the look of a human face, which is very noticeable on some early photos.

HURSTPIERPOINT

THIS village had a male witch (the term wizard was not normally used in Sussex), as well as the more usual female. The man was a Mr Brayser, who was reputed to be able to bewitch horses so that they could not work or even move. The witch, Mrs Still, was nicknamed 'Dame Prettylegs'. She was also able to stop horses from working when she felt like it, and she could put a spell on her neighbours to prevent them from getting home at night if they upset her.

KIRDFORD

A LEGEND from Kirdford tells how a local witch put 'the evil eye' on a young girl who had aroused her jealousy. The girl grew paler and paler and appeared to be wasting away. A wise woman, or white witch tried to cure her, but without avail. One night, the girl slept soundly – the first time for several weeks. In the morning she did not wake, but her cheeks grew rosy and her breathing became even. News reached her mother that the witch had died the previous day, so she allowed her daughter to sleep away the curse. After two more days the girl awoke naturally, refreshed and well with no recollection of her earlier state.

LEWES

THE very atmosphere of this old East Sussex town seems to speak of history and tradition. Several legends tell of anchorites, those strange religious hermits who were allowed to live lives of peaceful solitude close to the churches they loved. The cell of one such lady was discovered, complete with her bones, at St Anne's church, and it was said that St Richard left her a gift in his will, as well as similar bequests to other Sussex anchorites.

Another Lewes anchorite was Magnus, who was said to be a member of the royal family of Denmark, who had relinquished his rank for the life of a lonely hermit. It is not clear exactly who he was, but legend says that he was the son of Harold (by his second wife, Githa, a Danish princess), or that he was even Harold himself, who survived the Hastings battle, and chose to hide himself here until his death at 100 years old, when he disclosed his secret to King Henry I. The church he chose was that of St John-sub-castro.

Anchorites differed from other hermits, in that they stayed put in one place, usually a very small cell attached to a church, whereas hermits sometimes moved about and were not necessarily holy men or women. In spite of what must have been a very frugal life, in cold and darkness a good deal of the time, they lived to good ages and were considered an asset rather than a liability by their chosen churches.

In Anne of Cleves House at Southover, there is the table from East Malling, which according to legend, was chosen by the murderers of St Thomas a Becket to receive their arms after they had committed the dreadful deed.

Becket himself had often used this table, and after it received the blood-stained weapons it began shaking so much that they were thrown to the ground. After they were replaced, it again started to shake, in spite of being very heavy and firmly fixed to the ground. The top of the table is a massive slab of Sussex marble.

A more light-hearted story comes to us from the railway building era. A neighbour of an old lady went to a well to draw water for her, as her kitchen water pipe was frozen up. The good man lowered the bucket until he felt a jerk, followed by unearthly laughter from the well shaft. He ran back to the cottage exclaiming: 'The Devil is in the well!' The cause was soon discovered. The bottom of the well had been cut off by the excavation of a rail tunnel. The jerk was caused by a huge lump of chalk falling into the bucket, and the roar of laughter was from some of the excavators who were responsible.

LINDFIELD

MISS Helena Hall, the Lindfield historian, told of the Witch Inn, which she said had formerly been known as the Wych Inn because of a wych elm which grew outside the building. In spite of this commonplace explanation for the name of the inn, it did not prevent a legend circulating that years before a witch had lived close by. The story was that she had stuck pins in the footprints of those who had been there, in order that they should return and partake of a further drink before leaving for good. One is left wondering if she had some financial interest in the inn at that time.

John Halsham in his book about Lindfield *Idlehurst* (1898) said that the only belief in the occult he could find in the village was the reputation of Widow Blackman as a poor ghost of a witch 'only credited with the power to wish away warts'.

A hotel in Lindfield is supposed to have been haunted by the ghost of an old woman dressed in black in the style of the 1920s. She was seen going through the contents of a chest of drawers, with papers being thrown on to the floor. When the electric light was switched on, the whole scene, old lady, drawers and all completely disappeared, only to reappear a second time when the light was extinguished. The young lady who witnessed this worked at the hotel, and asked to be moved to another room; a request which was granted, although nothing was said about the apparition because of the possible effect on the guests.

LOXWOOD

A ROBED figure staring into space has been seen here by several people. It has been conjectured that the apparition might be that of a monk from a former monastery at Drungewick Manor, or a former owner of the manor house. A number of accidents have been noted on the road near to the sighting of the figure, and these have been connected in some people's minds with the apparition.

MAYFIELD

MAYFIELD, which has been called 'the sweetest village in Sussex' has several legends connected with St Dunstan. The saint was born at Glastonbury in AD 955, becoming famous as a scholar, craftsman, blacksmith, painter, musician and bell maker.

As Archbishop of Canterbury he seems to have adopted Sussex as his favourite county, building a palace at Mayfield. He also lived here as an anchorite in a simple hut, when he grew bored with the secular world. Legend says that the Devil tempted him one day in the guise of a beautiful girl. St Dunstan, who was enjoying himself at his forge, fashioning a chalice, recognised the Devil by spotting a cloven hoof beneath the folds of the damsel's dress. He seized the evil one by the nose with his blacksmith's hot tongs, and Devil, pincers, saint and all took off across the valley, where a great combat took place. The Devil managed to break loose, and took off with one great leap to Tunbridge Wells, nine miles away. Once there he plunged his smarting nose into the springs, giving them their distinctive flavour. Glastonbury also claims this miracle, but at least Mayfield has the saint's tongs and anvil as evidence. His hammer was also said to remain at one time, but this appears to have vanished. Tongdean is pointed out as the place where the tongs fell off the Devil's nose as he flew towards Tunbridge Wells.

When the church was being built at Mayfield, the Devil constantly moved it whilst it was in process of construction. St Dunstan was of course more than a match for his old adversary, and every time the Devil moved the church, the saint put his shoulder to it and pushed it back into place.

Although he had enemies, St Dunstan is remembered as a great statesman. He built and restored churches and worked on manuscripts and music. He died in AD 988 much revered.

Middle House in Mayfield was much admired by the author Arthur Beckett. He was told that Queen Elizabeth slept here when she visited the village. Also that it was haunted by the ghost of a lady, who was imprisoned in a little top room by her drunken husband while he seduced another woman in a room below. One day he was so drunk during his merry making, that he forgot to lock the door when he took food to his poor wife. So she found an iron bar, and when he appeared the next time, she hid behind the door and felled him. He rolled down the stairs, and his wife escaped. All of which doesn't actually explain why she came back to haunt the place.

MIDHURST

ONE of the great many Sussex legends connected with the Devil, is that he saw the five barrows on the summit of Treyford Hill and amused himself jumping from one to another.

The god Thor who was asleep nearby was disturbed by this activity, and told him to go away. The Devil taunted him, and then flung a rock at him, catching him in the midriff. Legend is silent on how Thor proceeded to exact his revenge.

NEWHAVEN

THERE are many good stories and legends about millers. This one is about William Coombs, who once had a mill near Newhaven. He was well known as a character, and once on a whim is supposed to have painted his horse yellow, then green and finally blue.

One day he made a rather contentious statement, and when it was contradicted, he swore that if it was not true he would never enter his own mill again. When it did indeed prove to be completely untrue, he kept his word, and for the rest of his life directed work within his mill from the top of the mill steps.

Another story about Coombs, which would appear to be even less likely than the previous ones, is that on his way to be married, a voice from heaven called to him 'William Coombs. If so be that you marry Mary, you'll always be a miserable man'. Coombs told this tale himself, adding 'And I be a miserable man!'

One more story about this singular miller, although there are others: one day when he was riding his horse (the unfortunate beast who had been painted all the colours of the rainbow), it was pointed out to him that with his own considerable weight, plus several sacks of flour, the animal was much overloaded. The miller assured the speaker that he wished to be merciful to his beast, and straightaway lifted one of the sacks onto his own shoulders.

NINFIELD

SID Neve who grew up in Ninfield, has given me several good stories and legends concerning the place. One was about a double grave in the churchyard, which was of two brothers who were one day scything wheat, when a violent quarrel broke out over the girl they both loved. In the scuffle that followed, one brother decapitated the other with his scythe. The former was hanged, and the two bodies were buried together in the same grave. As a boy he was told this story, of the 'Cain and Abel' grave, by the church sexton.

Sid remembered the wise woman of the village, who

was known simply as Mitch. Although there was a resident district nurse, the villagers had absolute faith in Mitch and when summoned she would immediately drop what she was doing and hurry on foot to the person who needed her, at any hour of the day or night. Whenever a villager complained of deafness, she would syringe out his or her ear, and she was always on hand when there was a football or cricket match to deal with such things as a dislocated arm. She never asked for payment, but of course her grateful clients in due course would leave at her backdoor an occasional rabbit, or some fruit or vegetables.

Although she would have been the last person to call herself a white witch, her great reputation was as a wart charmer. Sid Neve, with some little acquaintance with chemistry was sceptical of her powers, until one day his cousin's hands were seen to be covered with about a dozen warts. He consulted Mitch and she said to him: 'In four days they will be gone'. That's all. And they went – to his joy and amazement.

NORTHCHAPEL

HERE there once lived a man who was a poacher, drunkard and thoroughly bad lot, who was always ready to claim that he feared neither God nor the Devil. One Saturday night he was even more drunk than usual, and when the landlord of the pub tried to send him home towards midnight, he swore he would not go home, adding 'May the Devil burn me if I do'. This he repeated several times.

He was nearly 60, and must have drunk in the course of his life an immense quantity of spirits, in fact it would be true to say that he was rarely sober.

His companions, not quite so far gone as he, decided to drag him into a small adjoining room. They did not trouble to take any light with them, and there was no fire burning there. They loosened his neckcloth, and left him snoring on the floor.

Early on the Sunday morning, the landlord entered the room and was overpowered by an awful smell, of something akin to brimstone. There was nobody there, but in the middle of the floor was a heap of black ashes, which proved to be greasy to the touch. Of course the door had been locked, and there was no chimney and only a very tiny window.

They gathered the ashes with a shovel and buried them in the churchyard. The verdict was that this was a visible sign of God's anger, or the Devil responding to the poor man's wishes.

PARTRIDGE GREEN

PROBABLY Partridge Green's best known ghost story is one that really wasn't. The old Jolesfield windmill struck fear into the hearts of many country folk, who had to pass it after dark. There were tales of a ghostly figure, possibly that of a miller of years gone by who had been murdered. Then there were dreadful noises emanating from inside the mill, including screams and hissing sounds. One local insisted that he had seen a huge white something floating around the cap of the mill.

Certainly the mill had an air of eeriness and melancholy about it, and it was very easy to believe the stories that were told, and more besides. However, it must be said that many level-headed people believed that the only ghosts there were a pair of white owls who lived in the cap of the mill. Owls on their nocturnal flights must be at the bottom of a number of country tales of ghosts and hauntings.

PATCHAM

A CLASSIC ghost tale from the *Sussex Weekly Advertiser* in 1796. A particular spot in the grounds owned by Mr John Pain at Patcham, was for several years visited by what were described by the newspaper as 'supernatural appearances which greatly alarmed some respectable persons'. The sights were talked about, and many people would not pass that way at night. The restless spirit, it was noted, was particularly active on Christmas Day each year, when it was seen by several people who positively denied that it could be due to imagination. The sequel came in 1796 when some men were digging out a dyke on Mr Pain's ground, and came upon a skeleton about 18 inches beneath the surface. The bones were conjectured to be that of a female who had been brutally murdered, and then buried to cover up the crime. This story was borne out by the memory that 13 years previously a bundle of woman's clothes had been found in a field of corn near the same spot, by Mr Grover of Brighton.

The story does not conclude as is usual, with a note that the remains were given a Christian burial, but we can safely conclude that this took place, and presumably the ghostly appearances then ceased.

PETWORTH

MANY weird and wonderful stories and legends appear in the book *Tales of Old Petworth* which consists mainly of memories of Mr J O Greenfield during the early part of the 19th century. However this story goes right back to the 1760s, when there was an old woman known as Butter Ede. The children all believed her to be a witch, and would prove this by making a cross on the ground with straws or sticks, which would then force her to make a detour, rather than pass along the road bearing the cross.

At one time a local girl was apparently bewitched by

Butter Ede, so her employer (who must also have been a bit of a witch) decided to put matters right with some more witchcraft. He got a horse's heart, and stuck pins all over it, at the same time saying the Lord's Prayer, whilst nobody spoke. Then the witch's name was written on a piece of parchment, and this was stuffed into the heart, which was finally burnt to a cinder on the fire. The ashes were thrown into a stream of water which ran towards the witch's house. The girl is said to have recovered.

At the witch's funeral, the lightness of the coffin was remarked upon. A great black cat who had been her constant companion acted in a very wild way, running in and out of her house, and nobody saw it again after the day of the funeral. As the coffin was brought out, something was seen flying out of the kitchen chimney, accompanied by lightning, thunder and the smell of sulphur.

From the same collection comes a much more cheerful story about when Petworth church had a belfry and a clock was inserted in it by George, Lord Egremont. As there were to be four faces to the clock, he proposed that the townsfolk should contribute to the expense. Mr Sockett, the rector, objected to this. When Lord Egremont heard of the rector's refusal to contribute to the clock, he said 'Well, in that case Sockett shan't see what o'clock it is'. The eastern face of the tower, which looked toward the rectory, remained for several years without a clock dial.

PEVENSEY

A HUGE stone at the western boundary of Pevensey, was traditionally thought to have been brought there by an old woman as her contribution to the foundations of Pevensey Castle. She was carrying it in her apron, and at this spot her apron string broke, down went the stone, and there it remained.

PLUMPTON

MARCUS Woodward, writing in 1938 of his grandmother, Susannah Stacey, mistress of Stantons Farm, told of a local witch at Plumpton. She was reputed to be 100 years old, and extremely rich, with houses and lands. She often spoke of a hidden bagful of gold coins. Mr Woodward recalled as a boy being chased by the witch, who was running backwards, waving a knife and shouting incantations.

She would tramp the country for miles around, singing, dancing and ringing little bells. Like most other witches she was reputed to turn into a hare at certain times. She could easily cover 20 to 30 miles in one day, collecting herbs in a great basket she carried. Mothers used the mention of her to frighten children into being good, and even her name would strike fear into their hearts.

Some attempts to photograph her were made, but these were unsuccessful until one day a photographer succeeded by hiding in some shrubbery as she passed. (I wonder what happened to this photo?) Her trips took her into Brighton, where her figure was well known.

She often played the usual witch's trick on waggoners, by stopping their wagons as they tried to pass her door. She would then jeer at their attempts to make their horses move. One carter determined he would get even with her, so one day when the usual thing happened, he took out a large knife and cut notches on the spokes of his wheel. The wagon then moved, and the witch came screeching out of her cottage trailing blood from cuts on her fingers, one for every notch in the wheels. As it is well known that witches are afraid of cold steel, it is surprising that this sort of retaliation was not tried more often.

PORTSLADE

MRS Ethel Powell, who was brought up in Portslade, had some pleasant memories of her great-grandmother, who was known as Granny Rumney. As the local wise woman, she assisted the old doctor in ministering to the country folk who were her friends. When she was called, away she would go, striding out on her long legs, as she was very tall. When the roads were muddy (as Sussex roads so often were) she would wear pattens, which increased her height by about two inches. The small boys failed to appreciate her fine qualities and would chant after her:

Here's Granny Rumney,
on her pattens,
Fast as she goes,
her tongue goes clacken.

POYNINGS

AT the foot of the Downs there is a small piece of water which was known as the haunted pond or pool. The tradition is that a boy could be seen walking along the bank of the pool, wringing his hands in agony, or even jumping into the pool without making a splash.

The true story behind this ghost story is that in 1883 three boys were bathing, and two of them got out of their depth. The third boy ran to Poynings church for help, just as the congregation were assembling for evening service. The poor boy was so upset by what he had to communicate, that he completely lost his power to speak, and in panic returned to the pool just in time to see his two companions drown. It is said that this so upset him, that he died of melancholia soon afterwards, and has since continued to return to the site of the tragedy in spirit form.

PULBOROUGH

AN old country belief is that bees swarming on a dead stick foretell a death. This was instanced in the mid 19th century, when a woman at Pulborough was expecting a baby, and came upon a swarm of bees settled on a dead hedge-stake. She was convinced that what she had seen was a death token, and that she would die in her confinement. Her husband and even the village nurse both agreed with her, and a few days later the woman died – the husband saying that this was only what he had expected.

RODMELL

IN spite of the popularity of church bells, there are some people who cannot appreciate the beauty of the art of change ringing. The miller of Rodmell continually cursed even the single bell of the local church; in fact he cursed the bell, the bell ringer and even the blacksmith who made the bell in the first place. When his own curses proved powerless to silence the bell, he sought the aid of the local witch whose solution was to give him the impossible task of tying a hair from the Devil's tail to the clapper of the bell.

Beaten, the miller eventually grew to tolerate the sound of the church bell, although probably not to actually enjoy it. Years later he found himself completely lost on a winter's night, in one of the thick drifting sea-fogs for which the area was renowned.

After wandering aimlessly for some time, he was much relieved to hear the sound of the Rodmell church bell, and by following this he found his way home safe and sound. As a thanks-offering he paid for a new chime of bells for the church.

A nice story, only slightly spoilt by the knowledge that Rodmell is not the only place which has a legend of this kind.

RUDGWICK

AS we have seen there are a number of places in Sussex which have legends attached to church bells and water, in fact similar tales crop up in nearly a dozen different areas. A. Hadrian Allcroft has suggested that as large church bells (which feature in all these legends) were a relatively late introduction, then these stories, if they really are of any great antiquity, must surely relate to small Sanctus bells, which might well have been hidden to avoid them falling into profane hands.

The legend of the Rudgwick, Alfold Dene, Nowhurst or Slinfold Bell, is surely one of the most commonly told traditional tales in all Sussex. The setting is actually the same, although the name of the village varies according to which village the storyteller comes from. Many older folk have told me at least part of this story, and unlike many other Sussex legends which now survive only in written form, this tale is still being handed on by word of mouth.

The basic form of the story concerns a large bell, cast in Rome, that was being taken by boat and wagon to either Rudgwick church, or, in another version, York Minster. It rolled off the wagon and fell into a swamp or pond at Dedisham Manor Farm, near Rudgwick. A later attempt to raise it with a team of white heifers was unsuccessful, and it slipped back into the water where it remains to this day.

One of the best accounts comes from Mr Stephen Peacock, a retired farmer, when at the age of 78 he talked to a reporter from the *West Sussex Gazette* in 1965 relating the story which had originally come from an old carter, Pete Greenfield, who once worked at Dedisham Manor Farm:

> 'They went to a cunning 'ooman (a witch) and she told them that if they got twelve white oxen and went to the spot at midnight, they could rescue the bell. But no-one was to say a word. So one night they went with the twelve white oxen, which they hooked on to the bell in the bog. Then just as the oxen drew the old bell to the top, one of the men shouted 'We've got Alfold Dene gurt bell, in spite of all the devils in Hell'. At that

moment the chain broke, the bell slipped back, and they never got it after all.'

Mr S D Secretan of Rudgwick, writing in the *Sussex County Magazine* in 1943, had a similar account from John Pullen, one of the bell ringers of Rudgwick church, who died in 1931. He said that it was one of the bells of Rudgwick church which was buried in the marshy ground near Roman Gate, on the north side of the river Arun, west of Stane Street. It was being taken to Rudgwick when it rolled into the swamp. Someone said they would need white oxen to drag it out, but no-one must speak whilst this was being done. Of course someone spoke, and the devils gave an extra hard pull and the rope broke.

Another version from a man named Edwards who died about 1933 aged 90 or more, included the witch, but spoke of the bell being raised on a tripod with chains. It was when they were trying to slide a plank underneath it that one of the men exclaimed 'In spite of all the devils in Hell, we have got the Alfold Dene great bell'.

Alfold Dene is the name applied to a bridge crossing the Arun about a mile and a half from Slinfold, near where the old Roman Road (Stane Street) joins the main Horsham to Rudgwick road. This corner is most often referred to as Roman Gate, and the wooded area on one side of the road as Roman Woods. Until recent times the ground thereabouts was particularly boggy. There is however a village on the Surrey border, not too far away, which local people refer to as 'Arfuld' although it is spelt 'Alfold'.

The slight variations in the story as told by different people are interesting, although it should be noted that the basic facts always remain the same. The version which actually mentions Rudgwick seems to be the most common.

RUSPER

AT Rusper is the site of an ancient priory. In digging the foundations for new buildings, many graves were discovered – presumed to be those of the prioress and some of the sisters (several valuable relics were also discovered). The remains of the nuns were re-interred in Rusper churchyard, and a tablet fixed to the outside of the church as a memorial.

There is an old well known as the Nun's Well. Tradition states that the old bell of the convent was sunk in the pond at the front of the house, disappearing in the mud, in spite of attempts to retrieve it. There was also said to be a tunnel connecting the nunnery with Sedgwick Castle, near Nuthurst. Here there was also a well, constructed of large blocks of hewn stone. This was also known as the Nun's Well, or St Mary's Well.

In 1987 it was reported that the Star inn, at Rusper, was haunted by a ghost who had been seen as a shadowy figure sitting on a stool in the main bar. Other strange things happened, such as the beer being turned off half way through the evening, and the lights being extinguished.

RYE

WATER kelpies are mythical creatures not normally associated with Sussex. However, L Grant in his book *A Chronicle of Rye* (1926) tells the story of a courting couple who went walking one evening with their dog. They were in a field when a strange creature, like a horse with the face of a man, and with great staring eyes, came galloping past them. The vibration of the creature's hooves seemed to shake the earth, and when the man tried to encourage the dog to go after it, the animal was transfixed and would not move. So the young man left his girlfriend and followed the strange creature, in time to see it jump a tall fence, and into a large deep pool.

There was a long history of witches and their deeds in Rye. In 1571 Mother Margery, a poor old woman living in the almshouses, was driven out of town because she was thought to be a witch. It was said that she could cast a spell on good red meat, which would cause it to decay, and at the same time bewitch the person who owned the meat. After the old crone had been driven out of the town, it was noted that the troubles ceased.

That is until 1594, when Mother Rogers was accused of bewitching a child. A wise man advised the mother to draw the blood of the alleged witch, and so break the spell.

In 1608 there was a long drawn out case concerning witchcraft. Mrs Anne Taylor, who was described as a 'gentlewoman' was imprisoned on a charge of having 'councell' with evil spirits, although she was ultimately pardoned.

In 1645 the Mayor of Rye ordered the wife of Stephen Bruff and a widow, Ann Hoswell, both suspected of being witches, to be thrown in the river as a trial. This sounds a bit like the ducking stool, which some places in Sussex were known to use.

On another occasion, Joan Bayly, an 80 year old wise woman, told the wife of Thomas Hart, a Rye fisherman, that her child was bewitched, but that she could have the spell removed. She told the mother to fetch 60 needles, a halfpenny worth of pins, and a piece of red cloth. Into the cloth she stuck the needles and pins, and then put it on the fire. She then stuck a dagger into it, and explained that the witch would be drawn into the house. Unfortunately no one came, and the cloth was consumed by the fire. The case was considered by the Mayor and Jurats (municipal officers of the Cinque Ports), but no action was taken.

The best known ghost story of Rye has been well chronicled, but because of the unusual aspects of the tale, it seems a pity to leave it out of this book. It tells of a young monk with a most exceptional singing voice, who was unfortunate enough to fall in love with a lovely young girl who literally lived next door to the monastery. There was a connecting door from the monastery grounds into her father's garden. A devout Roman Catholic, he allowed the monks to come and go into his own grounds, as their own were somewhat limited. The young monk who is always referred to as Cantator, saw Amanda when he was on his daily walk, and was completely overwhelmed by her beauty. Soon they began meeting regularly and eventually this led to a decision to run away together. Their plan was discovered, they were pursued, caught, and a dreadful punishment on the monk was decreed. He was to be bricked up alive in his cell, and after this deed had been carried out, the lovely Amanda quickly joined him in death, expiring it was said of a broken heart.

But death did not stop the two lovers meeting, and they continued to do so in ghostly form. The monk tried to serenade his love, but because of the dreadful crime he had committed in breaking his vows, he could only make horrible gobbling sounds, more like a turkey than a gifted singer. The girl, who had been denied Christian burial, and her lover continued to meet in spectral form, in a spot which became known as Turkey Cock Lane.

In 1785, which was said to be nearly 300 years after the event, her ghost appeared in the form of a parrot, one of many forms she was supposed to inhabit. There have been other sightings of both Amanda and Cantator, even up to relatively modern times.

SEAFORD

LIKE Yapton, this place was also said to be the place where people originated from who didn't shut doors. But unlike the West Sussex village, there do not seem to be any stories to back up the saying.

There is a rather uncomfortable little legend about a house known as Corsica Hall, which stood on the site of an old mill. Later it was renamed The Lodge, but was still known as Corsica Hall by the older people. In the 18th century it was occupied by Francis, fifth Lord Napier. In the month of May 1772, one of his sons took up a loaded pistol that had accidentally been left on the table by Rev Loudon, his Lordship's domestic chaplain. Aiming it at the cleric, the boy said 'shall I shoot you?' The reply, said laughingly, was 'Shoot on'. The child did so, and Mr Loudon fell dead on the floor.

For some time afterwards the house bore an evil and unlucky reputation, and it was a long time before a tenant could be found for it.

SELSEY

ARTHUR Beckett, the Sussex author, wrote of Selsey:

St Wilfrid sailed to Sussex and he come to Selsey Bill,
An there he built a liddle church upon a liddle hill,
He taught the starving pagans how to net fish from the sea,
And then he them convarted all to Christianity.

This refers to the legend of St Wilfrid, who was born in Northumbria in the 7th century. Bedevilled by political problems at home, he travelled to Sussex, and landed at Selsey. A drought at the time had caused a famine, and the saint taught the natives how to fish – although this does seem a little unlikely when speaking of a population living on the coast. More usefully perhaps, rain fell soon after his arrival, and this helped St Wilfrid to persuade the Sussex folk to forsake their pagan ways and convert to Christianity. At Selsey he built a monastery and a church, and for four centuries this was the cathedral church of Sussex. Now the church has been swallowed by the sea, although at low tide it is said the bells in the steeple can still be heard.

Another church replaced the sunken cathedral in the 13th century, and the chancel of that church became the chapel at Church Norton. The 19th century church of

St Peter at Selsey utilised some of the stone from the earlier building.

Rudyard Kipling recounted a legend of Eddi, one of St Wilfrid's priests, in his book *Rewards and Fairies*. Although it was midnight at Christmas, the tale runs, none had come to the mass at the little church at Church Norton. But Eddi went on to celebrate the first mass of Christmas with just a donkey and a bullock as his congregation.

SHOREHAM

IN the early years of the 19th century there lived in Shoreham a country carrier, John Moorey, who was well known as a wise man, being able to cure such afflictions as ague, colic, dyspepsia, lumbago and tic. He was also credited with the gift of prophecy and second sight.

A poem was written about Shoreham's John Moorey, and his gift of second sight:

While John described the sights he saw,
As he did drive along,
Which quickly struck these friends with awe,
Whom he did mix among.

Strange sights on earth, strange sights at sea,
And stranger still in sky,
Which unto him did oft appear,
And sometimes very nigh.

I do remember well, a tale,
John Moorey once did tell,
Of scores of ships all in full sail,
That in the clouds did dwell.

And so on for several more verses, telling of Moorey's vision of Nelson's Battle at Trafalgar.

Henry Cheal who tells us about John Moorey in his *The*

Story of Shoreham (1921), also mentions a Shoreham witch, Molly Lawn, but unfortunately does not give us any information about her.

SLINDON

THE best known Slindon ghost story is about a riderless white horse, which gallops through the woods, and then just disappears as suddenly as it appeared. Many observers have reported this apparition, always at around the same place. It has also been several times reported that riders on horseback have found their own beasts stop and refuse to carry on, or else bolt for no good reason.

Another story is of the ghostly sounds of galloping horses, although there is nothing to be seen. One walker felt the rush of their passing, but at the same time appeared to be completely alone.

Another eerie Slindon legend concerns an old tramp who had never slept a night in a building. One day a lady who knew him slightly, was out riding when her horse stopped dead. All she could see ahead was the old tramp standing quite still. Suddenly he disappeared and her horse moved again. A week later a neighbour told her that the old fellow had died a few weeks before – not due to illness, but of a broken heart as he was about to be moved away from the Sussex Downs that he loved.

A strange saying in Slindon, if you do something foolish, is that you are 'as bad as Jack Inkster, who burnt half Slindon down'. Behind this saying is what one might term a local legend, although Jack Inkster really lived. As a puny boy he was sent from London to Slindon to improve his health. One day, acting like any typical boy, he chased a rat down a hole, and then tried to smoke it out. To do this he stole some sulphur matches from the smithy, and lit some straw. The barn caught fire, and then the rest of the farm buildings, followed by many other nearby thatched cottages and outhouses.

The Slindon police constable put him in the lock-up, and the next day at Arundel he was tried by the magistrates for wilful arson. Transportation was one of the punishments suggested, but because he was too small to even see over the front of the dock, the magistrates decided he was 'too small to punish'.

Priests are often featured in ghost stories, possibly because of the deep spiritual forces which occupied their minds when enacting the ritual of the mass, and also sometimes because they appear to have left undone tasks which they ought to have undertaken. This would seem to be a possible explanation of the priestly ghost which Bishop Wilberforce claimed to have seen in the library of an old Slindon house. When the bishop asked the priest if he could help him in any way, the ghostly visitor took him to a bookcase and indicated a paper inside one of the books. Guessing that this was the reason for the priest's unrest, Bishop Wilberforce burnt it on the fire. We are told that from that moment, the priest was not seen again.

STEYNING

ST CUTHMAN is undoubtedly one of the most popular of the early Sussex saints. Most of the details concerning him and his connections with Steyning, come to us in the form of legends. His birth was said to be in either the South or West country around the 9th century. As a boy he worked as a shepherd, amazing his contemporaries with simple miracles. At some time in his adult life he decided to set out with his mother in a handcart, looking for a place to build a church. On the way some mowers in a field laughed at him, and he caused a shower of rain to fall upon them, although it was a fine day elsewhere. His cart broke down at Steyning and here he decided would be the right place for his church. He toiled alongside the followers he had gathered around him, working several miracles in the process, such as his ability to hang his gloves on a sunbeam before starting work.

On one occasion a roof beam of the church was out of place and defied all efforts to set it straight. A complete stranger appeared from nowhere and, setting his shoulder to the beam, straightened it without difficulty. When one of the builders asked his name, he replied 'I am he to whom you build this church'.

The simple wooden church was later replaced by one of stone, and in turn by the present Norman church of St Andrew. An old gravestone is believed by some to be the site of the saint's last resting place. The legend of St Cuthman has been woven into a charming play by the author Christopher Fry.

Steyning once had a female anchorite, Miliana, who lived in the 13th century. Unlike most of her kind, she is traditionally supposed to have been positively belligerent, falling out with other holy people at every opportunity. She sued Richard of Hardham, a fellow anchorite, for some rents which she said he owed her. She then sued the Prior of Hardham for food which she said was due to her – this was supposed to amount to 5,600 loaves of bread 5,600 messes and 6,800 gallons of ale, all of which she claimed had been withheld from her for 18 years. The historian Mr Salzman said 'one wonders what would have happened if the Prior had admitted liability and dumped the whole lot outside her cell'. Afterwards she is supposed to have gone to law on several more occasions, but of course the whole account has been strongly denied by those who prefer likelihood to legend.

TANGMERE

IN 1984 at Tangmere's RAF Museum, it was reported that there had been three ghostly sightings of an airman in RAF uniform. In addition, objects had been moved about mysteriously, and a face had been seen looking out of a window after dark.

The theory offered was that it could be the ghost of an airman shot down, trying to communicate something. Some people also claimed to have heard the sound of a lone aircraft flying over the station during bad weather.

TURNERS HILL

MRS Ethel Powell told me the tale of how next door to her grandfather's cottage, there lived a family who ran foul of the matriarch of a band of gypsies, who roamed the woods and lanes of the area. The gypsy queen called down a curse on the whole family, saying each child should be born in some way defective – and so it was. One boy had a club-foot, another lad a defective spine, and one of the daughters was only 3ft high, although she had the head of a normal sized adult.

Her grandfather was quite a character, and when he went round to the big houses to pick up the table leavings for his pigs, he used a contraption like a big barrel on wheels, with shafts for his pony. He rode on this, and the children called him 'the King of Turners Hill'. Grandfather would sweep off his hat, bow graciously to right and left and flourish his whip. Once he allowed the pony to stray along the roadside, eating the grass at the edge. The local policeman took him to court. Grandfather agreed that he was guilty, and the magistrate fined him five shillings. As he took out his old leather purse to pay the money, he remarked 'I am grateful, Your Honour, I thought at least you would have hung me, and I never could stand anything tight around my throat'. The beak rapped out 'Ten shillings for Contempt of Court'. But Grandad said it was worth it.

TWO MILE ASH

THERE are two legends attached to the inn at the little hamlet of Two Mile Ash, near Southwater. The name of the hostelry is Bax Castle, and an oft repeated tale is that it was named after the composer Sir Arnold Bax, who lived in the area. This is supposed to have happened because he supplied it with whisky during the war, when supplies were short. Not so, as the inn had its distinctive name long before the famous composer came to these parts, and in any case the place did not even have a spirit licence until 1957. The story seems to have been accepted, as Bax spent the last years of his life living in another Sussex inn.

The other legend is attached to the unofficial name of Bax Castle, which for many years has been Donkey Bridge, The Donkey or just The Donk. The story behind this is that the original owner, whose name actually was Bax, and who was a weaver, owned a donkey which he tethered in front of the building. During a very bad spell of weather, the animal was found dead one morning having frozen to death. Some of the local lads propped up the frozen donkey, and it stayed that way for two weeks, much to the amusement of the locals. This does seem to be a reasonable explanation for the patrons of the inn to start talking about 'going down to The Donkey', so this may be one legend with a good deal of truth in it.

UDIMORE

ST Mary's church at Udimore was begun on one side of a stretch of water, but each night the work disappeared completely. Some of the villagers sat up and watched and listened, and afterwards described how the air was full of the rushing of wings of angels, who were carrying the building materials across the water, chanting 'Over the Mere, Over the Mere'.

So the builders took the hint, and the church was built where the angels wished. This has an even more unlikely sequel, in the theory that the name of the village, Udimore, evolved from the angels' chant of 'Over the Mere'. There are of course other more plausible origins for the name.

This is one of the many Sussex legends that tell of how churches when they were first built, were moved by supernatural forces (sometimes devilish, other times as at Udimore, angelic). It has been conjectured that these legends originated when the early Christian church builders erected their churches on what had been pagan sites, and perhaps suffered interference by enemies of the church.

WARBLETON

HERE was an ancient priory, which later became a farmhouse. In 1413 when Hastings Priory was in danger of being swamped by the sea (which did actually happen), Sir John Pelham gave the monks this site. One room was said to have an indelible bloodstain on the floor, where an unfortunate man was said to have been pinned to the boards with a sword and left to die in agony. There is also the legend of two skulls which had to be left in the house. Any attempt to bury the skulls resulted in horrible noises at night, and the death of cattle in the adjoining fields. One day someone is supposed to have removed the two skulls and placed them in an apple tree, where a tit took up residence – using the eye sockets as a means of entrance and exit. No consequences of this act are noted. One old lady held the skulls in her lap for over 20 minutes, and said afterwards that she felt all kinds of horror and fear – which was hardly surprising. The reasons behind the legends have not been explained.

WARNHAM

A LOCAL legend says that nearly 200 years ago a young soldier who had been crossed in love, hanged himself, and was therefore buried in unconsecrated ground, by the crossroads. It was said that the grave was constantly supplied with fresh flowers, although no one was ever actually seen tending it. The soldier was a stranger in the village, so presumably had no relatives there. The vicar at the time decided that the flowers were placed on the grave due to some local superstition, although it was also conjectured that it was gypsies who placed the flowers there. At one time it was suggested that the mound marking the grave should be levelled, but this was not proceeded with.

Another version of the tale is that it was a cattle stealer's grave, and the thief was hanged on a tree near the crossroads. A hole was dug underneath, so that the body could be lowered straight into the grave. The man who told this story said that it was children who put flowers on the grave, and that a road maintenance man, Sugar Woodman, trimmed it once a year.

WEST CHILTINGTON

LEGENDS say that this was the spot where the last wolf was killed in Sussex. The exact place was known as Wolfscrag.

In earlier times wolves were very plentiful in the county, and in Norman and Plantagenet days a reward of five shillings per head was paid for their slaughter. Pretty good pay at that time, for the killing of what were termed vermin. They continued to roam wild until the reign of Henry VII, but tradition is silent as to exactly when the last Sussex wolf was killed.

WEST DEAN

MRS Charlotte Latham in her collection of West Sussex superstitions of 1868, quotes a groom residing in this village, who, when speaking of the local witch, said there was no way that one could resist her power: 'If she willed that I should sit across the roof of this stable from morning to night she'd have me up there in an instant, and nothing could bring me down till she gave me leave to come'. This is the lady who was never spoken of by her neighbours except as 'The Witch'. All dreaded her power, and every misfortune that befell them was put down to her influence, but rather than say that they were bewitched they would use the expression 'sin-struck'.

Another informant told me that a cottage in West Dean once had a bottle full of pins on the hearth. Visitors were told not to touch it as it was red hot. The woman of the house explained that her daughter suffered from epilepsy, and the local doctors were unable to help her. She had consulted a wise woman, who had told her that the daughter's fits were due to witchcraft. The red hot pins were to prick the heart of the witch who had cast the spell and force her to remove it, so that the daughter would be cured.

WEST TARRING

HERE it was that legend says St Thomas a Becket, Archbishop of Canterbury, had his palace (now a hall), and also a fig garden. A different legend tells us that it was St Richard of Chichester who brought the fig trees over from the continent.

We know that the gardens were in existence in 1745, although some of the trees are said to be much older than that. By 1830 the 100 trees were producing 2,000 figs in a year. An additional legend says that this garden and another in Sompting are visited each year in fig time by a bird similar to the beccafico (figeater) of Campagna, Italy. In Victorian times there was an entrance charge of tuppence to view the fig trees. In 1990 there were newspaper reports that only about two dozen of the 100 trees were left, due to development of the site.

WINCHELSEA

A CLASSIC tale, which exists in many different forms, comes to us from Winchelsea. There was once a man who hoarded his money in a chest. One day when he looked at it, he saw a little black demon sitting on the box. It exclaimed 'Begone. This money is not thine, it belongs to Godwin the Smith'. Not daring to use the money himself, he decided nobody else should have it. He put the box in the hollowed-out trunk of a tree and threw it into the sea.

It was carried to the door of Godwin, who dwelt in Rye. Thinking it would make a good yule log, he put it in the fireplace and on Christmas Eve it was lit. The heat melted the coins in the box and the metal ran out. His wife noticed this, and hid the precious metal.

Helped by his wife, Godwin became rich and the Winchelsea man was forced to beg from door to door. The story became known, and when the beggar asked for alms at Godwin's house, his wife, smitten with guilt, baked him a loaf hiding a quantity of money in it. The miserly man took it, and on his way home sold it unbroken to some fishermen for one penny. Godwin's wife saw them about to feed the loaf to their horses, and substituted oats instead. So the miser remained poor.

There just has to be a good moral in there somewhere.

WORTHING

SOME people believe that dogs have the ability to anticipate the death of humans, particularly those they love. The Victorian newspapers thought they had a very good story of this sort, when it was reported to them that a Newfoundland dog owned by a Worthing clergyman, had laid down one night on the steps of a house in Warwick Street. He refused to move, and howled continuously. A young lady residing in the house was ill, and later died that night. This was pointed out as uncanny proof of the dog's ability to foretell a death – until the clergyman mentioned that the dog had become lost during the day, and after running about in search of him, had finally settled on the steps of the Warwick Street house where his master had frequently called.

I am not sure what eventually became of Worthing's 'Weeping Angel' which had a brief period of fame in 1961. This was a Victorian painting which had been found by a man shortly after he moved to a new address. The picture, which was discovered in the garage, was of angels announcing the birth of Christ to the shepherds. The new owner was astonished to find that one of the angels appeared to be weeping, and he became convinced that there was something miraculous about it. He placed the picture first on one side of the fire in his lounge, and then on the other, but in spite of the warmth, the eyes of the angel still expressed tears, and the tears tasted salty. A drop was taken away by a museum official for analysis. Neighbours who also saw the picture confirmed the owner's story.

A short time after this the owner said that he was intending to burn the picture. I wonder what did happen to it.

YAPTON

A TRADITIONAL saying still current today is that if you don't shut doors you must come from Yapton. One reason put forward is that a Yapton farmer had a calf which got its head stuck between the bars of a gate, and to free it he cut off its head. He then decided that henceforth all his gates must be left open.

Another tale runs that to avoid window tax, a gentleman had most of his windows blocked up, making his house so dark that the servants had to leave as many doors open as possible. But I really prefer the tale of a great black dog which haunted the village. The doors were left open to allow it to pass through, and not to worry the villagers by howling at the lack of entry. (Surely a supernatural dog could have passed through the doors anyway!) My informant's mother often talked about the 'howling of the black dog'.

SUSSEX DIALECT

NO book which touches on Sussex dialect, however slightly, would be complete without some attention being paid to the man whose name will always be closely associated with the study of the ancient words and sayings of the county.

William Douglas Parish was ordained to the church in 1859 and, after serving as curate at Firle for four years, was offered the vicarage of Selmeston and Alciston. At that time these villages must have been about as remote and unspoiled as it is possible to imagine. But Parish was not content to minister to his country folk, although he obviously did this exceedingly well, for he also became chancellor of the Cathedral of Chichester, and the first chairman of the Sussex Archaeological Society. He evidently had a tremendous love for the children in his parishes, and wrote poetry for use in elementary classes and became a school inspector.

Some of the best anecdotes about him, and there were many, are contained in a book published in 1912 by a fellow Sussex parson, the Rev Edward Boys Ellman, Rector of Berwick. He mentions several examples of the sense of humour possessed by his friend and neighbour. Once when he asked him to subscribe to the Clergy Widows' Fund, he refused on the grounds that he was already helping the society by not marrying. One of his few failings was a complete lack of musical appreciation. One day when he was at work in the library at Chichester Cathedral he was bothered by the sound of the organ, which he thought was being tuned. When he asked a verger to go and ask the man if he could put off his tuning until he had finished studying, he was informed with some ruefulness that an organ recital was taking place.

Writing in the 1930s, the Rev A A Evans described Parish as an 'original', and commented that among the parsons of Sussex, there was no one quite like him. In the country area in which he lived and worked, one might expect a certain dullness and monotony, but Parish brought his own particular liveliness with him wherever he went, and the vast range of his interests may be judged by the books he wrote, which even included a manual of instruction on the electric telegraph, in addition of course, to his dialect dictionary.

When Evans was writing in the 1930s, Parish's *A Dictionary of the Sussex Dialect*, which had been published in 1875, could still be bought for a few shillings; although now the original editions fetch many pounds, always assuming one can be found. Apart from the evident scholarship within the book, it is also a very readable and entertaining work, as he was not content to merely list dialect words, but was at pains to illustrate how they were used. Just one example – under *Peert* he gives the illustration 'Baby do seem better – she'm more peertlike'.

Before Parish compiled his dictionary, there had been as far as I know, only one earlier attempt to do something similar. This was *A Glossary of the Provincialisms in use in the County of Sussex*, by William Durrant Cooper, which was first published in 1834 for private circulation. Parish's dictionary was an attempt to produce something much more comprehensive, but of course any work of this kind can never be considered complete.

As early as 1890 Miss Helena Hall of Lindfield and her brother John Henry Sussex Hall, had started to note Sussex words heard in their own district, which were not included in the Rev Parish's dictionary. In 1957, when the original book had been out of print for many years, she was able to produce a valuable augmented edition, including all the additional words collected by her and her brother, and also a fascinating section on Sussex sayings and crafts.

My own interest in Sussex dialect, may be said to have started when as a child I was subjected to these words and sayings every day of my life by my mother and aunts (and a lesser extent my father). All these expressions seemed part of ordinary life, until I went to school and discovered that not many other children (this was the late 1920s) knew what I was talking about, and I hastily began to revise my ideas as to what words could be used outside of the home circle, and what could not. Later I began collecting these words from memory, and also from other sources. A very minor contribution, compared to the work of the Rev Parish and Helena Hall, but I hope nevertheless that the brief glossary which follows, which includes many of the best known of Parish's words plus some not noted by him or Miss Hall, will interest those who have not previously been aware of the riches of our dialect. It may also encourage others to dig even more deeply into what is a most engrossing subject.

A Short Glossary Of Sussex Dialect Words

A-bear	To put up with someone or something; 'I never could a-bear him.'
A-bed	Lying in bed, perhaps due to illness.
Abide	To put up with something, used similarly to 'A-bear'.
Ackle	The working of machinery or tools; 'This should make it ackle'.
Ad-as-lev	'I would as soon as'.
Adle	Unwell; 'I feel rather adle today.'
Adone	Leave off. (Parish said that when a Sussex girl says 'Oh! do adone' she means carry on, but when she says 'Adone do' she means stop it at once.)
Afeared	Afraid; 'I'm afeared of that dog.'
Afore	Before
Agin	Close to; 'Put that agin the wall.'
All-one	The same; 'It's all-one to me whether you do it or not.'
Allow	To express an opinion; 'It'll rain afore nightime, I allow.'
All-manner	To describe something unsatisfactory, or to end a sentence.
Allus	Always
All-mops-and-brooms	To be in a muddle, a favourite housewifely expression.
Along-of	Because of; 'He slipped along-of the ice on the road.'
Amost	Almost
Anywhiles	At any time; 'You can see him there anywhiles.'
Arf	Half
Arney	In a bad temper; 'He's a birt arney today.'
Arts-and-parts	In all directions
Aslew	Slanted or out of true
As-lief	Similar to 'Ad-as-lev'.
Atween	Between
Atwixt	Between
Awhile or Awhiles	For some time; 'It won't rain yet awhiles.'

Awk	A big awkward fellow.
Axey	The ague, a much dreaded complaint in old Sussex.
Bacca	Tobacco
Bait	Farm worker's refreshment, such as bread and cheese (or fat bacon) and cold tea in an old lemonade bottle.
Ballet	A ballad or song, as sold by a street vendor on a penny sheet.
Balsam	Uncomplimentary remarks; 'That's enough of her old balsam.'
Bandy-ann-day	Monday, the day when cold leftovers were eaten.
Bannick	A beating; 'He deserves a good bannicking.'
Banyan day	The same as 'Bandy-ann-day'.
Bark	A bad cough
Barse-ackards	Back to front
Bat	A walking stick or some other piece of wood.
Bat and trap	A game played on Good Friday in Sussex, particularly in Brighton.
Beasted	Tired out
Beat the devil round the gooseberry bush	To ramble on without getting to the point.
Beazled	Tired out; similar to beasted but perhaps even more so.
Beer babies	Babies sired whilst the man was the worst for drink.
Beggar boy's heart	A very hard thing. Often I have heard my mother say 'that's just as hard as a beggar boy's heart', when something proved difficult.
Beggar's broth	See 'Kettle broth'.
Behopes	Let's hope; 'Behopes he wont be late'.
Beleft	Believe; 'I just cannot beleft it'.
Belikes	Likely
Benson's peg	The floor or the ground; 'Don't hang that on Benson's peg.'
Bettermost	Good quality
Betwixt and between	Between one thing and another.
Biggest land and the worst reap	Someone who is full of woe.

Biggest part of a tidy bit	A fair amount
Bile	To boil. To clean a watch you should 'Ile and bile it'.
Birchbroom in a fit	Description of someone of an unkempt appearance.
Biscuit	Often used in Sussex to mean a cake.
Bishop-Barnaby	The lady-bird. Used by Sussex children in the rhyme: *Bishop, Bishop, Barnaby,* *Tell me when my wedding shall be.* *If it be tomorrow day,* *Ope your wings and flyaway.*
Bittenous	Something liable to bite, like a fierce dog.
Bittle-battle	The game of stoolball, very popular in Sussex.
Black-man	An imaginary monster, sometimes used to frighten children.
Blackeyed-Susan	A Sussex pond or well pudding.
Blackthorn winter	A cold snap at the time of the Blackthorn blossom (March).
Block ornaments	Butcher's scraps.
Boco	A large amount. Probably from the French, but often used by my mother, preceded by 'much'.
Bodge, bodger	A careless way of doing a job, and one who was therefore not considered a good worker.
Bon	Very good, again probably from the French, and popular with my mother and aunts.
Bostal or borstal	A steep path up the side of a hill.
Bottley	Round glass marble, taken from the neck of a ginger beer or lemonade bottle.
Brave	In good health.
Breechy	Description of bitter water.
Broom dasher	Parish gives the older meaning of a dealer in brooms. In my family it meant a roughly dressed, roughly spoken person, 'He's a proper ole broom dasher'.
Brown George	Large apple turnover (at least 18 inches long).
Brung	Brought
Bum-freezer	A very short coat.

Bunt	A blow or push.
Burny	Dry and brittle, such as soil.
By-the-bye	Accidentally or by chance.
Cabbage	To copy from another's work, as in an examination.
Cackhanded	Description of an awkward person.
Cad	An inferior who helps you in your work.
Caddling	Looking around for odd jobs, or leaving a job half-done.
Cadger	A beggar.
Call	Cause; 'There's no call to speak to me like that'.
Called over	Reprimanded
Cannons	A game in which marbles are rolled along the gutter.
Cardinly	Accordingly
Carroty	Brittle and crumbly wood.
Cart	Left in the lurch; 'He left me praply in the Cart'.
Cat and conjure	Game, see 'bat and trap'.
Caterwise	Diagonally
Catlicks	Roman Catholics
Catterning	To solicit for apples or money on St Catherine's Day.
Cavings	Ears raked off the corn when it is threshed.
Chank	To chew.
Chastise	To correct or verbally abuse someone, rather than to physically punish.
Cheese-cutter	A conker with a flat edge, also a flat cap.
Chipe	Prolonged talk or chat.
Chipper	Happy, cheerful.
Chuckle-headed	Of low intelligence.
Chuff	Miserable, surly. (Unlike the modern term 'chuffed' which means just the opposite.)
Chummy	A felt hat as worn by farm labourers in old Sussex.
Church-yarder	A bad cough.
Chutter-dump	A rubbish dump.
Clemmed	To be very hungry, cold or miserable.
Clobber	A set of clothes or other belongings.
Close view of the floor	A spanking.

Cluck	Parish says 'Out of spirits' but in my family it meant the opposite, 'to be self satisfied' in fact.
Clung	Cold and damp, particularly applied to damp washing.
Coager cake	A plain cake.
Cochel	A volume measure – too much for a wheelbarrow and not enough for a hand cart.
Cocker-up	To invent a story.
Coddy	Small and neat.
Cojer or Coger	Meal of bread, cheese and beer.
Cold as charity	Very cold.
Come-by-chance	An illegitimate child.
Conk	Old piece of machinery.
Consarned in liquor	The worse for drink.
Contrairy	Obstinate; typically Sussex, where the natives 'wunt be druv'.
Countable	Very; 'He is countable tight-fisted'.
Cowman's bedsocks	Cord or strap tied by a farm labourer just below the knee, to raise his trousers. (Also called by many other terms.)
Cow-pat	A cow's droppings.
Create	To make a fuss; 'Don't keep on creating so'.
Cross-ways	Where four roads meet.
Crow	To swank or boast.
Cut your stick (or cut your hook)	Be off straight away, you are not wanted.
Dabs	Game of knuckle-bones. See also Dibs.
Dabster or dab-hand	One who is good at a game or a particular skill.
Dabtoe	A nuisance or a pest.
Daft cuddy	A simple person.
Daisy cutter	Penny-farthing cycle.
Dame	Respectful title given to aged married woman of the working classes, often a widow.
Dang	Alternative for Damn or something even worse.
Dare	May; 'They dare to go inside'.
Darn-ma-wig	Expression of surprise.
Darter	Daughter

Dasent	Clean and decent.
Deaf adder	Slow worm.
Deedy	Parish says 'Clever; industrious', but I remember it always being used in the sense of 'quiet and deep in thought'.
Delser	A small neat thing.
Dentical	Picky or choosy.
Devil	Black lamb in a flock – considered lucky.
Devil dodgers	Those who go to church in the morning and chapel in the evening, or the other way about.
Devil's box	Church organ or harmonium, or any musical instrument such as a concertina or melodeon.
Devil's children	Magpies
Devil's dancing hour	Very late at night.
Devil's prayer book	Pack of playing cards.
Dezzick	A day's work.
Dibber or Dibbler	A pointed wooden tool used for making holes to sow beans, seeds etc.
Dibs	Game of knuckle-bones. See also Dabs.
Dick	A ditch or trench.
Dick or Dickie	A small boy whose name is unknown.
Didicais or Diddies	Gypsies
Dido	A mix-up, or some kind of trick.
Dinlow	Slow witted.
Dishabill	Disorder; 'My room is in a terrible dishabill'.
Dish of tongues	A telling-off.
Ditch water	Something dull or miserable, as in 'dull as ditch water'.
Dobbers	Marble game. See Cannons.
Dobbs or Master Dobbs	A fairy who helps with the housework.
Doddle	A slow walk.
Doddle to-and-again	To walk to and fro.
Dog tail	Running about or getting in the way. 'Don't dog tail all over my clean floor'.
Dog-tired	Tired out.
Dolly	A figure made out of straw.
Dollop	A lump of something.
Donkey tea	A drink made by crumbling toast in water.
Doolah-tap	Silly or drunk.
Dorm	To move about in an irritating manner.

Dosset	A small portion.
Dowly	Dreary
Dozzle or dossle	A small article.
Dracly	Directly; I'll do it dracly', which might mean 'anywhen' in the future.
Draggle-tail	A sluttish girl.
Drinted or drented	When colours run in the wash.
Dripped-pudding (or dropped pudding)	Sussex suet pudding made to eat with the Sunday roast.
Druv	Driven, as in the Sussex motto 'we wunt be druv'.
Duck's frost	Rain rather than freezing.
Dumbledore	Bumble bee.
Dungpot	Dung cart.
Dunnamany or dunnamuch	Not to know how many or how much.
Dunner	To be outdone.
Dursnt	Must not; 'He dursnt do that again'.
Dyke	A bank or earth wall, although it is also used to apply to a dick (or ditch). Also used to mean a WC.
E'en-a-most	Almost
Effet	A newt.
Elynge	Weird or lonely.
Faggot	Parish says 'A good for nothing girl'. My mother used it to mean anyone who was annoying or troublesome.
Faggot above a load	Too much of a good thing, or as in 'He hasn't got a faggot above a load' to mean someone who was very poor, but tried to pretend he was well off.
Fairy loaf	Fossilised sea urchin.
Farcey	Overeating
Fardy	Interrupting; 'Stop poking your fardy in'.
Farisees	Fairies
Fat Jack	A fat, or perhaps just an annoying person.
Fettlers	Railway plate-layers.
Fidgety britches	A very worrying person.
Fill-dick or fill-dyke	To fill with rain as in 'February fill-dyke'.
Fives	See Dabs.

Fla'ed Isaac	Unkempt person.
Flag basket	Woven from sedge.
Fleed cakes	Cakes made with pig's fat.
Flit or flittermouse	A bat.
Flowering	To go out gathering wild flowers.
Follow-after	Marble game. See Cannons.
Foreigner	Anyone who is from elsewhere; even another village.
Fraidy-cat	A coward.
Frap	To hit.
Freed	Cold; 'It's very freed today outdoors'.
Frenchy	A foreigner.
Frit	To be frightened; 'I was very Frit'.
Frouden	To be frightened.
Fur my heel	To annoy; 'She really did fur my heel'.
Furrin	Foreign, even somewhere but a short distance away.
Furs bush	The tune that cats sing when they purr.
Fust	First
Gammy leg (or any other joint)	An injured leg, or limb.
Geat	A gate.
Gellish ornary	To be ill. 'I feel gellish ornary today'.
Generally always	Generally. 'He generally-always does it that way'.
Gentleman	Someone who does not need to work for their living. Can be applied to an invalid or even a pet.
Gifts	White specks on the finger nails. Supposed to foretell a gift on the way.
Gill	Long strip of woodland with a stream in the middle.
Gimsy	Fashionably dressed.
Goblins	One of several possible calls after Good Friday (when the marble seasons ends) which meant that your marbles would be confiscated, if you still carried on playing.
God Almighty's cow	Ladybird
Goistering	Loud feminine laughter.
Gooding or goodening	The old custom of going to the big houses for gifts towards the Christmas feast, on 21st December (St Thomas's Day).

Goodman	An old form of address for the man of the house.
Goody	An old form of address for an old widow.
Gowk	A cuckoo, therefore a fool.
Grammered (in dirt)	To be very dirty.
Gravel rash	Marks, usually on the knees, caused by falling on a gravel road or path.
Grisping and griping	Continually complaining.
Grunter	Misaligned course of brickwork.
Gurt or gert	Great. 'He was a gurt big fellow'.
Gutter alleys	Marble game, see Cannons.
Gwain	Going
Hagridden	To have a nightmare.
Hagtrack	Circles of brighter green grass, said to be tracks of witches or fairies who have danced there at night.
Halve	A long chat; 'We had a really good halve'.
Ham	A grass plot.
Hanger	A wood on a hillside.
Happen-along	To meet by chance.
Hard dick	Sussex pudding, made only with flour and water.
Hark tack	Poor food.
Hasty pudding	Pudding made with bay leaves and eggs in milk.
Have	To take. 'I'll have her home in no time'.
Hayt	Sussex carter's command to pull.
He	A name for the Devil. Also the main player in a Tag game.
Heave gate	A Sussex gate that lifts out, instead of opening in the usual manner.
Hedge carpenter	A rough and ready wood worker.
Hedge-pigs	Hedgehogs
Heft	To lift.
Hem	Euphemism for an expression such as Hell.
Higgler	A hawker or travelling salesman.
High-lows	Shoes, something between shoes and boots.
Hill	The Sussex Downs.
Hind	A labourer or servant.
His'n	His own.
Hobblyguts	Omnibus

Hogboat	A fishing boat peculiar to Brighton.
Hoggings	See Goblins.
Hoggle	To fall.
Holt	Hold; 'She took holt of me'.
Holy Sunday	Easter Day.
Horn-fair	Rough music, with pots, pans, horns etc, intended to show social disapproval of a neighbour who has been guilty of bad behaviour. (There is an annual Horn Fair at Ebernoe, in Sussex, on July 25th.)
Howlers	Boys and men who wassailed the fruit trees around Epiphany.
Huckle-bones	Bones used for playing Dabs or Dibs.
Huckle-my-buff	Beer with eggs and brandy.
Hugger-mugger	In a mess.
Humbledores	Hornets
Huvver	Fluffed up, as birds in cold weather.
Ibidioy	A lout.
Ikey	Proud, haughty.
Illify	To accuse someone of evil.
Innards	The stomach.
Itching berries	Rose hips
Jacks	See Dabs.
Jacks or Jack-hearns	Herons
Jackdaws' parliament	Many people talking at once.
Jacket	To give someone a good telling-off; 'I'll jacket him if I catch him doing that again'.
Jack on the pinch	Making use of someone.
Jack-up	To give up, or stop work.
Jambreads	Slices of bread and jam.
January butter	Sussex mud.
Jaspers	Sussex fishermen.
Jawmedead	A great talker.
Jib	Someone's manner or style; 'I liked the cut of his jib'.
Jigger	A harmless oath.
Jipper	Gravy
Joe Bassetts	Larvae of the Chafer Beetle.
Jobal	Jovial
Joe and 'Arry	Bread and cheese.
Jollop	Gravy
Jonnick	Pleasant, approachable.
Joram	A large bowl.

Josser	An old fellow.
Joutering	Useless argument.
Jug	Brighton fisherman.
Jugglers	Brighton fish carriers.
Jump up (or round) and hang by nothing	To do something in a hurry.
Justabout	Certainly
Justly	Absolutely right.
Keeps a good length	To keep a good garden.
Kettle bender or kettle broth	Bread with pepper and salt, soaked in hot water, and eaten like bread and milk. (My Grandfather's breakfast every day of his life.)
Kettle wedges	Small pieces of wood suitable for the fire.
Kicks	A marble game which involved throwing a marble against the side of one's boot to make it rebound.
Kiddle or kittle	To tickle or tease.
Kiddy	A friend, workmate or other un-named person.
Kissing crust	Soft crust formed by pulling apart a cottage loaf.
Kissing gate	A gate which can only be used by one person at a time; and therefore a boy could neatly corner a girl and exact a kiss.
Kite	An untidy person.
Kittle	Kettle
Knab, nebb or knep	A small hill.
Knuckesholes or nuckesholes	Springs which are reputed to be bottomless.
Laines	Open tracts of land at base of the Downs.
Lame	Any injury to arm or leg.
Lamentable	A popular Sussex adjective meaning 'very'.
Lanky-tom	A very tall person.
Lapsy	Slow or lazy.
Lardy-johns	Flat cakes made of pastry.
Larn	To teach, and sometimes to punish.
Larrup	A thrashing.

Latchety	Working badly.
Lather or leather	To thrash.
Latten	A sheep bell.
Laurence or Old Laurence	A mysterious person who makes one lazy; 'Old Laurence has got hold of me today.'
Lawyer	Brambles, also called Sussex-lawyers.
Lay	I believe; 'This will make him jump, I lay.'
Layovers and catch-meddlers	Contents of bag or basket.
Lear	Parish used this to describe 'Thin, hungry, faint.' My mother who was very fond of the word, used it to imply a feeling of emptiness in the pit of the stomach, rather than just normal hunger.
Leben	Eleven
Leavebe	Let me.
Leaze	Land on which the right of pasturage applies.
Leg	A long strip of land between woods or fences.
Leg-bail	To get away quickly; 'I'll leg-bail as quick as I can'.
Let be	To leave alone.
Levenses	Mid morning snack.
Libbet	A stick used for knocking fruit out of trees; also used for throwing at cocks, and at squirrels when such activities were considered sports.
Licker	Something which takes a lot of believing.
Liefer	Sooner; 'I'd liefer go this afternoon'.
Like	Often added to the end of a sentence.
Lil-ole	An adjective for almost anything.
Linger-and-die	Horsham to Steyning railway line.
Lippy	Saucy
Liversick	A hangnail.
Loiter-pin	Applied to a lazy person; 'He would make a loiter-pin to wind down the sun'.
Lone-handed	Single handed.
Longanner	A tall person.

Long hook	Long time to wait; 'My money is on a long hook'.
Long rope day	Good Friday; from the custom of skipping on this day.
Looby	Slightly soft-headed.
Looker	A shepherd; used in East Sussex.
Lord John (or Old Johnny)	The ague.
Lord Tom Noddy	An important person, at least in their own estimation.
Lot, lote	A pond.
Loute	To bend.
Loving mud	Sussex mud, because 'It do cling so'.
Low	Allow or conclude; 'It's a lovely day, I low'.
Lubbock	Big ungainly person.
Luddick	Something which has fallen down.
Lurgy	Lacking in energy.
Magnify	Matter; 'It don't magnify one way or t'other'.
Maid	Young children of either sex.
Main	Much; I'd be main pleased to meet you'.
Malook	Mad or daft.
Marble day	Good Friday, from the custom of playing marbles until mid-day.
Marestails	Streaky white clouds, said to bring wind.
Mariandums	Marks instead of actual writing.
Master	Old name for a married man; also used by wives when speaking of their husband.
Mawk	Teenage girl.
May-be, mayhap	Perhaps
Mazed	Bewildered
Meece	Mice
Melancholy	Much; 'A melancholy fine lot of onions'.
Mermaid's purses	Egg cases of the dog fish.
Messpot	A dithering person.
Middling	A word with several meanings, often used when the speaker does not wish to commit himself; 'How are you today?' 'Middling'.
Miller's glory or miller's pride	Windmill sweeps set in the sign of a cross, which is supposed to bring good luck.

Mind	Remember; 'I mind him very well'.
Min Upton's lil ole Will	Used instead of a name which you cannot recall.
Miriander	A happy halfwit.
Mis or Mus	Shortened form of Mister.
Misagree	To disagree.
Miserable	Mean
Miserable as sin	Very sad.
Mislike	Dislike
Mister Grim	The Devil. (One of his many Sussex alternative names.)
Mistus	Mistress; often used by a Sussex man when speaking of his wife.
Misword	A cross word.
Mixen	A dungheap.
Mizmaze	Confused state.
Mock-beggar-hall	A house or farm where the food and furnishings are very poor.
Moggy	Barn Owl.
Moithered	Bothered, bewildered.
Monkey's birthday	When it rains and the sun shines at the same time.
Mongst the middlin'	Fairly well.
Month of Sundays	A long and boring time.
Monstrus	Very much; 'A monstrus big catch'.
Morris or morrising	To dance.
Mort	Many
Mortal	Very much; 'It is mortal cold today'.
Most-in-ginral	Generally, usually.
Mousearnickle	A dragonfly.
Mouzle	To crumple up.
Mumpers	Tramps
Murphy	A potato.
Mush-faker	Poorly dressed person.
Music	Any musical instrument, but particularly a concertina or melodeon.
Muther-wut	Carter's command to a horse to turn right.
Mutton barracks	Valley near Telscombe noted for its sheep population.
My obediance	A mother's name for her first born child.
Nary	Not any; 'Nary a one'.
Naughty man's plaything	Stinging nettle.

Naythur	Neither; 'Naythur one nor t'other'.
Near	Miserly
Neat	Exact
Nestle	To fidget.
Nettle	To annoy.
Nettle beer	A drink made from nettles.
Nims	Cords worn below the knees to keep the trousers away from the mud.
Nineways for Sunday	To look bewildered or surprised.
Nipper	Young boy.
No chicken	Not so young.
Nollegers	Straps to hold the trousers up away from the mud.
No nation thing	Expression of scorn.
Not blown away	Not short of cash.
Nottable	Thrifty
Nuzzle	To nestle.

Obedience	A bow.
Ockerd	Awkward
Old apple woman	A ditherer.
Old Clem	A figure dressed with beard and pipe, and set over the place where the blacksmiths held their St Clement's Day feast (November 23rd).
Old faggot	A nasty person.
Old fashioned	A suspicious look.
Old fashioned touch	Old style person.
Old Grist (as fat as)	A very fat person.
Old Steere's pig	Answer to question 'Who said that?'
Old Tom Pepper (as big a liar as)	Very great liar.
On	Of; 'I tried to grab hold on 'em'.
On pins	To be very worried.
Oration	A fuss.
Ornary	Unwell, out of sorts.
Orts	Bits and pieces.
Othergates	Other ways.
Othersome	Other times.
Otherwheres	Other places.
Otherwhiles	Other times.
Ourn	Ours
Outermost	Greatest
Overlay	Oversleep in the morning.

Over Will's mothers	Tucked away in some place. Also used to indicate direction of impending weather.
Owler	Smuggler
Paddle	To walk around indoors with muddy shoes.
Painful	Painstaking; 'A painful teacher'.
Painter's lunch	½ pint of beer and five woodbines.
Parley francy	To talk French, or some foreign language.
Particular	To appear unwell.
Passel	A large group, such as 'A passel of birds'.
Pawsy	Soft headed.
Peaked or peaky	Looking sickly.
Peck	A pick axe.
Peewits	Small marbles.
Peert	Lively and bright.
Peg away	To carry on working.
Personable	Charming
Perty	Pretty; 'It's perty close'.
Pesky	A nuisance.
Peter-grievous	Said of a whining child.
Pharisees	Fairies
Picksome	Hungry, also finnicky.
Pig	Misaligned courses of brickwork.
Pig-meat	Pork; 'Pig-meat pudding'.
Pig nut	Earth nut.
Pig sticker	A large knife.
Piker	A tramp.
Pill garlic	Something hot; 'I'll give him some pill garlic'.
Pimps	Bundles of firewood.
Pinch bottom day	29th May.
Pinchplumb	A mean person.
Pinchgut	Relieving Officer.
Plagey	Troublesome
Plaster for every wound	An answer for every situation.
Pleasuring	An outing.
Plum heavy	A round cake made of pastry with currants in it.
Poke	A sack and also put, as in 'You will have to poke up with it'.

Pond pudding — A Sussex pudding, also called 'Black-eyed Susan', or 'well pudding'.
Pooch — To pout and also to push.
Pook — A poke, also a fairy name.
Pooking-stick — Billiard cue.
Pook flies — Puck or fairy flies, said to worry cattle when they career across a field.
Poor man — One more name for the Devil.
Poor man's asparagus — Young shoots of bracken.
Poor man's treacle — Garlic
Poundnotish — Well spoken.
Prapper — Proper; 'I feel prapper poorly'.
Prensil or prensley — Presently, often used to mean at present.
Prickleback urchin — Hedgehog
Prodidogs — Protestants
Pucker — A fuss, also snatched with cold.
Puck stool — Toad stool.
Puff — A lifetime.
Pug up — Put a thing away safely.
Purling — Looking intently.
Puss net — Tangled string or thread.

Quality — The nobility.
Quarry — Small window glass.
Queer — To puzzle; 'It queers me to know that'.
Quid — A cud.
Quiddy — What did you say?
Quissby — Unsettled weather.

Rackon — Reckon; 'I rackon he's a good kid'.
Rack-up — To give the horses their feed for the night.
Radical — Bad and troublesome.
Ragtush — An untidy person.
Rake — Word applied to the sea when it breaks on the beach with a grating sound.
Rake, as thin as a — Very thin person.
Ramp — To grow rapidly and well.
Rare — Good, plentiful; 'A rare lot of apples'.
Rat dick — Horsham name for the river Arun.
Raw throat — Sore throat.
Rawt and rawtun — Angry complaining by a woman.
Red headed dane — Term of reproach to a red-haired man.
Reynolds — 'Mus Reynolds' is a name for a fox.

Rheumatics	Applied to many different forms of rheumatism.
Rindy frost	Hoar frost.
Roaders	Tramps
Rook	To steal or swindle.
Rookery	A disturbance, or place where a crowd make a lot of noise.
Rough music	Sounds made by tin pans, horns etc to express disapproval against someone who has misbehaved.
Round frock	Usually used as an interchangeable word with smock, although strictly speaking the two are slightly different.
Rousers	Large fireworks used at Lewes on Bonfire Night.
Rovendens	Yet another name for the cord or strap used by the agricultural worker to tie up his trousers at the knee.
Rubbishy buster	A very untidy person.
Ruddles	Sticks of green wood interwoven between upright sticks to make a hedge.
Rumbler	A sheep or horse bell.
Rumbustical	Blusterous in manner.
Runagate	A good-for-nothing.
Runaway Jack	Ground ivy.
Running the hacks	Drying areas of new bricks.
Sad	Cake or bread which has not risen.
Sarternoon	This afternoon
Sartinly	For certain.
Scandalise	To insult someone.
Schmosell	A lot of noise or fuss.
Scorse	To swap or exchange.
Scrabbles	See Goblins.
Scritch owl	Barn Owl.
Scroopun	Whistling shrilly.
Scrumping	Stealing fruit from orchard trees.
Scrouging	Pushing
Scurriwinkle	To move furtively and quickly.
Sear	Burn or scorch.
Sere	Withered grass.
Sen	Since; 'I haven't seem him sen last Easter'.
Seraphim	Church barrel-organ.
Set-out	A mix-up; 'That turned out to be a fine set-out'.

Settle	A wooden bench.
Shab	To hurry.
Shackle	Thin vegetable soup. (Parish says to idle, and a thatching bond.)
Shackle-breeches	A slow, lazy person.
Sheeres	The rest of the country apart from Sussex and Kent.
Shepherd's crown	Fossil sea-urchin, often found on the Downs by shepherds.
Shim	A glimpse of someone, even a ghost.
Shimeroys	Gnats; 'They shimeroys do bite'.
Ship	Sheep
Shirty	Bad tempered.
Shock	A sheaf of corn.
Shoon	Shoes
Shooting alley	Large marble.
Shorn-bug	A beetle.
Short	Bad tempered. Also used for pastry that is very crumbly.
Shruck	Shrieked
Shut of	To be rid of something or someone.
Side hill	Hillside, particularly the Downs.
Skattle cat	Woman of sly, pilfering disposition.
Skidders	Piece of metal used by children to control a hoop. (Other similar words are also used - skiddaws, skellers, skeelers, skimmers.)
Skillings	Attics or low roofed rooms, sloping to ground.
Skin	Bad tempered; He's in a bad skin today'.
Slew-ways	Sideways
Slirrup	To suck up liquid, such as soup, noisily.
Slommocky or slummocky	Messy, untidy.
Slouch-puddin	Shambling walker.
Slyboots	Sly, devious person.
Smell of an oil rag	To give nothing away, 'I wouldn't give him a . . .'
Smugs	Another word which could be said at mid-day on Good Friday when playing marbles, allowing the speaker to confiscate the marbles.
Snag or sneg	Snail
Snags	See Goblins
Snirk	Dried up, withered.

Soon	Daft or slow witted; 'He is a bit soon'.
Spannel	To make dirty footmarks on a clean floor.
Spicket	Spigot
Spile	Spoil
Spirimawgus	Name used to frighten children; 'Ole Spirimawgus'll have you'. (Devon dialect has 'Spirimogle - a supernatural being'.)
Spotted dick or dog	A sultana sponge pudding.
Sprod	Junction of a branch with the trunk of a tree.
Spruse or spruser	To cheek or mislead, one who is sly.
Squeeze-belly gate	A narrow gate.
Squatetings	Female conversation.
Squack	Baby's cry.
Squimbley	Feeling queer or upset.
Srievelous	Very slow; 'He was a bit srievelous'.
Stampsies	If when playing Conkers, your opponent's conker falls to the ground without breaking, you may stamp on it and cry 'Stampsies'.
Starving	Shooting at birds; 'Rook starving'.
Steening	Lining a well with bricks.
Stone alleys	Stone marbles.
Stranger	A single tea-leaf floating in a tea cup.
Strick	Strike; 'I strick that note about right'.
Struttick	Nothing at all; 'He hasn't got a struttick'.
Suky	Kettle
Surelye	A very popular word in old Sussex speech, when it was often added at the end of a sentence to round it off. (Rather as 'you know' is so often used today.)
Sussex bomb or Sussex gumbo	Alternative names for Sussex pond pudding.
Sussex marble	Winklestone
Sussex moon	Lantern used on the back of a wagon, or carried.
Sussex pudding	A simple flour and water pudding.
Sussex weed	The oak tree.
Swanky	Light beer.
Sweal	Parish gives only the definition 'To singe or burn'. I have also heard it used to mean 'scour clothes'.

Swede-nawer (or Sussex swede)	An ignorant countryman.
Swimmers	Flat rounds of plain suet pudding, boiled and then served with butter and sugar, treacle or jam. Also used in my mother's family to mean any slightly unappetising dish.
Swipes	Light beer.
Swymy	Feeling faint or sick.
Tackle	Working tools or equipment.
Tackle-to	To start a new job.
Take-and-go	To make up one's mind suddenly to do something.
Tallyman	Door-to-door salesman who collects the cash week-by-week. Also used in hop picking.
Tantaddlings	Small jam tarts.
Tanty	Dainty
Tapsell gate	A gate working on a central pivot.
Tarade	A lot of noise or commotion.
Tarble	Terrible, much.
Tar-boy	Boy with the tar pot at sheep shearing, to use as an antiseptic on a cut. 'Don't spoil the ship for ha'porth of tar'.
Tarrify	Terrify
Taw	Large marble.
Tedious or tejus	Very; 'It weighed a tejus large amount'.
Terrible or tarrible	Excessively
Tessy and tiffy	Irritable
Thick of hearing	Deaf
Tibster	A small man.
Timmersome	Timid
Timnails	Vegetable marrows.
Tin-pot	Description of a self-important person.
Tipteers or tipteerers	Christmas Mummers.
Token	A gift. Also used to mean a ghost sent to warn of a death.
Tollard	Candle grease scraped out of flat candlesticks.
Toller	Tallow
Tolly	Shooting marble.
Top-of-the-house	Someone who has lost their temper.
Tottle grass	Quaking grass.
Trapes	To walk around.

Trip	To place something behind a wheel to stop it slipping.
Trug	A Sussex basket made of split wood, much beloved by gardeners.
Tumble-down-gate	A gate which is opened by one end being pressed down.
Twit	To tease.
Twitten	A path between walls, hedges or buildings.
Twizzling	Spinning a pointer on pub ceiling to decide who should pay for next round (or even to divide up smuggled goods).
Unaccountable	A popular Sussex adjective, meaning very or exceptional.
Unkid	Not made known.
Upright and downstraight	An honest, uncomplicated person. (Several times I heard this description applied to my late father.)
Upsides	Hard to best or get the better of; 'You jest cannot be upsides with him, nohows'.
Urchin	Hedgehog
Urr	Rough taste (such as quince).
Valiant	Well made, very much.
Varmint	Rascal, rogue.
Varn	Bracken
Varning	Collecting bracken.
Walloping	A spanking.
Water bewitched	Very weak tea.
Weeson	The throat.
Well mannered	Describing the growth of vegetables.
Well pudding	One of the many names for what is more often called Sussex pond pudding.
Wet	To make the tea.
Wet week	Slow or dispirited; 'As slow as a wet week'.
Whapple way	A bridleway.
Wheelbarrow	Used in place of an unpronouncable word.
Wheels	A hand cart or sack truck.
Whiffle	Coming in fits and starts.

Whistle and row (or ride)	Work while you talk.
Widdershins	Going contrary to the course of the sun.
Wig	Bun
Wild	The weald of Sussex.
Wimwams for goose's bridles	Something not understood.
Wittle	A fringed shawl used by countrywomen.
Woddle	The game 'bat and trap'.
Worsle or worslers	Wassail or wassailers.
Wounded beanstick	Tall thin person.
Wrastle	Wrestle, do battle with.

Sussex Dialect Counting

SHEPHERDS and other agricultural workers often used their own dialect words when counting in their work. Some families or farms had their own particular sets, although these might be similar to those in use by their neighbours. The usual set of counting words in use by Sussex shepherds was as follows:

One-erum, Two-erum, Cockerum Shu-erum, Shitherum, Shatherum, Wine-berry, Wagtail, Tarrydiddle, Den.

The sheep were counted in pairs, so Den stood for a score.

Mrs J Duggan Rees, in her 1988 book *Slindon: Portrait of a Sussex Village* quotes an old Slindon shepherd, George Bowley, with the following set of numbers - not unlike the above:

One the rum, Two the rum, Cocker rum, Shutter rum, Shether rum, Shather rum, Wim berry, Wig Tail, Darry diddle, Dess.

Another set seems to be lacking in some numbers:

Obery, Twoery, Tickory, Tebbon, Ollobone, Crackabone, Ten-or-eleven, Spin, Span, Must-be-done, Twiddleum, Twydleum, Twenty-one.

Of course some allowances must be made for tricks of memory, or pronunciation.

Here is one more set, which seems to be complete up to twenty. Each fifth word was accented, followed by a pause:

Wintherum, Wontherum, Twintherum, Twontherum, Wagtail. Whitebelly, Coram, Dar, Diddle, Den. Etherum, Atherum, Shootherum, Cootherum, Windbar. Bobtail, Inadik, Dyadik, Bumpit, Ecack-tally.

Similar sets have been noted from other English counties. And then there were the nonsense words used by children in counting games, such as this set noted in Sussex in 1935:

Ena, Deenah, Dinah, Doe.
Catterah, Wheelah, Whiler, Woa.
Coram, Doram, Pullem, Flea.

Acknowledgements

AS with all my other Sussex books, many people have helped me with this one. First of all my thanks to the following, who have contributed information:
Mr C Anscombe, Mrs M Bryant, Mr E Carley,
Mr C W Cramp, Mr P Gumbrell, Miss D Hall,
Mrs E Hallett, Mr F Holmes, Mr T Holmes,
Miss V Mercer, Mr A Moore, Mrs M Murray,
Mr S Neve, Miss M Page, Mrs E Powell, Mr G Stedman,
Canon W Stone, Mrs J Sunderland, Mr G Townsend,
Mrs F Tuts, Rev T Tyler, Mrs E Vincent, Mrs C Wales,
Mrs M Wales, Mr R Wales, Mrs W Whiting.

Some of the above have passed on, but I hope their inclusion in this list will serve as a tiny memorial to them. For those who I may have overlooked, and the many who have offered me items of value from their memories at talks I have given in various Sussex village halls, I also offer my heartfelt thanks.

Then there are the authors of the hundreds of Sussex books, articles and newspaper reports, which I have perused over the years; and the museum curators and librarians, who have never failed to respond to my requests.

To all of them – and my long suffering wife, who puts up with it all,

THANK YOU

Bibliography

Aitcheson, George *Sussex,* (1936)
Albery, William *A Millennium Of Facts In The History Of Horsham And Sussex* (1947)
Allcroft, A Hadrian *Downland Pathways* (1924)
Anderson, Elizabeth S (Ed) *West Sussex As Seen Through The Eyes Of The W.I.* (1975)
Arthur, Dave *A Sussex Life* (1989)
Austen, Edmund *Brede, The Story Of A Sussex Parish* (1946)
Austin, Janet *Kirdford – The Old Parish Rediscovered* (1990)
Axon, William *Bygone Sussex* (1897)

Beckett, Arthur *Adventures Of A Quiet Man* (1933), *The Spirit Of The Downs* (1909), *Wonderful Weald* (1911)
Belloc, Hilaire *The County Of Sussex* (1936)
Bishop, J G *A Peep Into The Past* (1892)
Blaker, N P *Sussex In Bygone Days* (1919)
Brabant, F G *Rambles In Sussex* (1909)
Bradley, A G *An Old Gate Of England* (1918)
Brown, Lilian *All About Bury* (1948)
Burke, John *Sussex* (1974)
Burstow, Henry *Reminiscences Of Horsham* (1911)

Charman, Aubrey *Southwater Through 200 Years* (ND)
Cheal, Henry *The Story of Shoreham* (1921)
Christian, G *While Some Trees Stand* (1963)
Cobb, Ruth *Travellers To The Town* (1953)
Coker Egerton, Rev John *Sussex Folk And Sussex Ways* (1892)
Coleman, S Jackson *Sussex In Vignette* (ND)
Cook, Greville *A Chronicle Of Buxted* (1960)
Cook, W Victor *The Story Of Sussex* (1920)
Cooke, Arthur Stanley *Off The Beaten Track In Sussex* (ND)
Cooper, William Durrant *A Glossary Of The Provincialisms In Use In The County Of Sussex* (1834)

Copper, Bob *Early To Rise* (1976), *A Song For Every Season* (1971)

de Candole, Henry *The Story of Henfield* (1976)

Ellman, Rev Edward Boys *Recollections Of A Sussex Parson* (1912)
Evans, Rev A A *On Foot In Sussex* (1933), *A Saunterer In Sussex* (1935)

Fairweather, Leslie *Balcombe* (1981)
Fleet, Charles *Glimpses Of Our Sussex Ancestors* (1st and 2nd series, 1882/3)

Geering, Thomas *Our Sussex Parish* (1884)
Gordon, Rev H D *A History Of Harting* (1877)
Grant, L *Chronicles Of Rye* (1926)
Green, Andrew *Ghosts Of Today* (1980)
Greenfield, John Osborn *Tales Of Old Petworth* (1976)

Hall, Gordon Langley *The Enchanted Bungalow* (1959)
Hall, Helena *Lindfield Past And Present* (1960)
Halsham, John *Idlehurst* (1898)
Hare, Augustus J C *Sussex* (1894)
Higham, Roger *The South Country* (1972)
Holmes, Edric *Seaward Sussex* (1920)
Hopkins, R Thurston *Cavalcade Of Ghosts* (1956), *The Lure Of Sussex* (1928), *Sussex Pilgrimages* (1927), *Sussex Rendezvous* (ND)
Hurst, Lady Dorothy E *Horsham. Its History And Antiquities* (1868 and 2nd edition, 1889)

Jennings, Louis J *Field Paths And Green Lanes* (1877)

Kaye-Smith, Sheila *Weald Of Kent And Sussex* (1953)

Latham, C *Some West Sussex Superstitions Lingering In 1868* (1878. Folk-Lore Records, Part 1)
Leigh, Rhoda *Past And Passing* (1932)
Leslie, Shane *Shane Leslie's Ghost Book* (1955)
Lower, Mark Anthony *Contributions To Literature* (1854)
Lucas, E V *Highways And Byways In Sussex* (1904)

Maxse, Lady *Petworth In Ancient Times* (1952)
Maxwell, Donald *Unknown Sussex* (1923)
McCarthy, Edna and Mac *The Cuckmere* (1981)
Mee, Arthur *The King's England. Sussex* (1937)
Meynell, Esther *Country Ways* (1942), *Small Talk In Sussex* (1954), *Sussex* (c 1940)
Middleton, Judy *History Of Hove* (1979)
Montgomery, John *History, People And Places In West Sussex* (1977)
Mundy, Percy D (Ed) *Memorials Of Old Sussex* (1909)

Parish, Rev W D *A Dictionary Of Sussex Dialect* (1875 and expanded edition by Helena Hall, 1957)

Roundell, Mrs Charles *Cowdray: The History Of A Great English House* (1884)

Sawyer, Frederick Ernest *Sussex Folk-Lore And Customs Connected With The Seasons* (SAC Vol XXXIII, 1883)
Simpson, Jacqueline *The Folklore Of Sussex* (1973)
Swan, William Carter *The Diary Of A Farm Apprentice* (1984)
Swinfen, Warden and Arscott, David *Hidden Sussex Day By Day* (1987)

Wentworth Day, J *Here Are Ghosts And Witches* (1954)
Whitlock, Ralph *In Search Of Lost Gods* (1977)
Wolseley, Viscountess *Some Sussex Byways* (1930)
Woodford, Cecile *Portrait Of Sussex* (1972)
Woodward, Marcus *The Mistress Of Stantons Farm* (1938)
Wright, Maisie *Cuckfield–An Old Sussex Town* (1971)
Wymer, Norman *Companion Into Sussex* (1972)
Wyndham, Margaret *Mrs Paddick* (1947)

Young, Colonel A Donovan *Titus Oates Lived Here* (1958)

The Petworth Society Magazine
Evening Argus
Sussex County Magazine

Sussex Archaeological Society Collections
Various Sussex guide books
West Sussex Gazette
West Sussex County Times
Sussex Life
Sussex Notes And Queries

INDEX